HOW TO BUY &
RUN YOUR OWN
HOTEL

Some other titles from How To Books

How to Run a Successful Pub

Starting and Running a Guest House or Small Hotel

Marketing for the Micro-business

Book-keeping and Accounting for the Small Business

Preparing a Winning Business Plan

How to Get Free Publicity

howtobooks

For full details, please send for a free copy of the
latest catalogue to:
How To Books
Spring Hill House, Spring Hill Road, Begbroke
Oxford OX5 1RX, United Kingdom
info@howtobooks.co.uk
www.howtobooks.co.uk

HOW TO BUY &
RUN YOUR OWN
HOTEL

*"...a brilliant insight to the hospitality business, covers all the bases
in a no-nonsense and practical style. Highly recommended for
anyone in or aspiring to ownership and management."*

MARK LLOYD

howtobooks

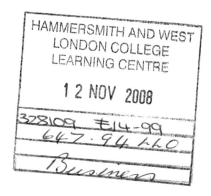
Published by How To Books Ltd,
Spring Hill House, Spring Hill Road,
Begbroke, Oxford OX5 1RX, United Kingdom.
Tel: (01865) 375794. Fax: (01865) 379162.
info@howtobooks.co.uk
www.howtobooks.co.uk

How To Books greatly reduce the carbon footprint of their books by sourcing their
typesetting and printing in the UK.

British Library Cataloguing in Publication Data
A catalogue record for this book is available from the British Library

ISBN 978 1 84528 275 2

Cover design by Baseline Arts Ltd, Oxford
Produced for How To Books by Deer Park Productions, Tavistock, Devon
Typeset by TW Typesetting, Plymouth, Devon
Printed and bound by Bell & Bain Ltd, Glasgow

NOTE: The material contained in this book is set out in good faith for general guidance and
no liability can be accepted for loss or expense incurred as a result of relying in particular
circumstances on statements made in the book. The laws and regulations are complex and
liable to change, and readers should check the current position with the relevant authorities
before making personal arrangements.

Contents

Preface   ix

1 So you think you want to own a hotel?   **1**
Understanding why you want to own a hotel   1
Considering whether your previous experience is relevant   2
Choosing the hotel that is right for you   4
Considering the bricks and mortar   11
What your friends/colleagues will tell you!   13
Starting with the practicalities   14
Qualifications – what you must have!   16

2 Being your own boss – the reality   **20**
Why is being your own boss so appealing?   20
Are you the right type of person/people to run a hotel?   22
How much fun/hard work is it really?   23
What qualifications do I need to run a hotel?   27
How running a hotel will affect you and your way of life   28
Knowing your strengths and weaknesses   29

3 The purchase – practical advice on the initial stages   **30**
Location, location, location   30
Financing your purchase – how much will it all cost?   33
Choosing the right finance option – who to turn to and who to avoid   35
Writing a business plan – what to include   38

Working out what you can afford! 50

What costs to expect when making the purchase 51

Running costs – your first month in a new business 57

Choosing a bank for your new business 57

4 Considering making a purchase **60**

What to look for when you first visit 60

What questions to ask the seller 70

What to consider before making an offer 82

Giving yourselves a reality check 83

5 Making an offer and what happens next **87**

Making an offer 87

What happens once the offer is agreed? 88

What about the vendors? 90

Reaching the point of no return – planning ahead 92

Managing the hotel before you move in! 97

Making the move – the big day 103

6 Preparation is the key **107**

Are you ready to run a new business? 107

What nobody will tell you! 110

Preparing for the unexpected 113

Employing staff 114

What you need to know about suppliers 121

Planning for your first few days 131

Who you will need to contact 135

You've arrived – what next? 139

7 A year in the life of a hotel owner **147**

Managing day to day – more of what nobody will tell you! 147

Dealing with customers – customer service is everything! 158

Managing communications   166

Managing your bank account – not learning the hard way!   172

Looking after yourself and your family   176

How life changes – by people who know!   180

Odd things can happen at any moment!   182

8 Diary of a hotelier   **184**

Daily time schedule   184

The schedule   185

Our story from the beginning   **202**

Appendix: An A–Z of practical advice   **211**

Index   237

Preface

At the age of 45 I had worked tirelessly for other people for long enough. I had become tired of dealing with the attitudes of people I worked for, most much younger than myself and in many cases with no practical experience whatsoever. I found myself becoming more and more disenchanted and dreaming of a different future!

This book is dedicated to all of the people that thought and probably still think that we were mad to make such a drastic change to our lives. More importantly, it is dedicated to all of you out there who are thinking of a similar venture. To some of you such a change will be just a pipe dream; to others it will be more than that – much more in fact.

There is no doubt that you will be desperate to change your routine and to work for yourselves. You will be spending progressively more of your time searching commercial property agency sites on the internet for that holy grail of hotels.

Once we had decided to make the change we began to look in earnest for a suitable property in a suitable location. When we found exactly what we were looking for, and had an offer accepted, we started to tell close friends and family of our decision.

With just one or two exceptions we received the same response: 'Are you mad? Running a hotel is extremely hard work.' We now realise that our reaction to this was completely defensive: 'How would they know? What experience do they have? I can't work any harder than I do now – how hard could it be?'

I would explain how I felt communicating this by simplifying what I thought would be involved: 'Guests book, they arrive and check in, they go to bed, have breakfast in the morning, pay and then leave.' How is that difficult in any shape or form?

We are now 18 months into our new 'way of life' and often look back at the time before we arrived and examine our progress. We frequently discuss our experiences and how our lives have changed.

At the time of the decision to bail out of our normal life I had searched the internet and local bookshops for any literature that could ease our passage and assist in running a totally new business. I was largely disappointed. I could not find anything that described what we were letting ourselves in for. I did discover a couple of excellent publications – these were textbooks giving hints and tips on what we needed to consider. However, they just didn't go far enough.

What I was really looking for was someone who could tell me what to expect based on his or her experience of running a hotel, something that was anecdotal, but that also gave solid and practical advice. This would give an insight into the daily routine of a hotel owner and would explain in detail what was in store for us. Nothing can prepare you for this way of life more than being in a position to tap into the knowledge of someone who has actually done the job.

I hope that our experience of the last 18 months, from when we first started to consider buying a hotel, through to actually running a small ten-bedroom hotel for nearly two years, will give you the best possible start, will prepare you for your new venture and will give you a first-hand account of what you can expect at every step of the way.

1
So you think you want to own a hotel?

Understanding why you want to own a hotel

When I decided I wanted to run a hotel I couldn't quite put my finger on the reason why, nor can I remember exactly when I decided this would be a good idea. I found myself trawling the internet for hours searching for 'Hotels for Sale' and spending days dreaming of what it would be like to leave the rat race behind and truly be my own boss. Each day I would spend more time looking for the 'perfect' hotel. I hadn't actually thought through what constituted the perfect hotel or indeed the perfect business – I just seemed to *know* what I was looking for.

It is now 18 months since we took over our hotel and, looking back to my days of searching, I realise that I did know exactly what I was looking for – and more importantly the reason why I knew. It must have been in-built – in my genes if you like – and I realise now that the hotel we found matches our personal requirements perfectly.

During the searching period I was also looking into my family history, starting with my grandfathers who had both died within three years of my birth. I discovered that one grandfather had run a hotel in Gloucester for five years and owned a public house in Denham. He had also run countless charity events at top venues in London. My great-grandfather had once been the manager of the Grosvenor House Hotel on Park Lane. In addition one of my great-grandmothers had owned a hotel in Scarborough. On top of all that, my sister now owns a hotel in Malaga.

Considering whether your previous experience is relevant

I also realised that my working background and experience had prepared me for what lay ahead. Similar to most people of my upbringing I started work at 16, initially as a clerical officer for the Lord Chancellor's Department followed by two years as a credit controller and a further five as an assistant accountant for an insurance broker. After this I moved to a company in London and started in the accounts department, first on bought ledger and then as credit manager.

I then had my first complete change in direction and trained in sales for the same company, selling exhibition space. After three years I took over as sales manager on an exhibition and progressed to sales and marketing manager. I left after eight years and spent a couple of years working for several different publishing companies and event organisers before becoming self-employed. Over a 15-year period I worked on hundreds of events, conferences, exhibitions and corporate functions and finally specialised in the management of Award Events.

All of these 'careers' prepared me for running a hotel. Over time I had gained experience in civil court proceedings, credit control, accountancy, sales, event organisation, project management, customer service and marketing. I had controlled an office of 20 staff and run sales and marketing teams. Additionally, for the last seven years I was self-employed, working from home running an event management business.

Looking at my future

So why did I want to run a hotel? This wasn't an easy question to answer when my friends and family first enquired. They started to question my sanity. I simply replied that 'I just did'. It was something that I knew I wanted to do.

I had also searched my soul and asked myself the same question. I looked into my future and just couldn't see myself organising corporate functions for another twenty years. During my later years of self-employment I met a man in his 60s who was consulting on event management and he gave me a glimpse of what I might become like if I didn't change.

I had already had a taste of what it was like to be my own boss. However, I still had to answer to clients, not every single day but at least once a week. I no longer wanted to be accountable to other people.

I had no idea what it would be like to run my own hotel. I really needed someone to tell me. If someone had it wouldn't have deterred me but it would have prepared me better than I could prepare myself.

If you want to change your life, your environment, your future, then buying a hotel and working for yourself is certainly an option. But you need to examine why you want to do this and what is involved.

I looked at hotels on the internet, investigated the different types of hotels, looked at locations, read magazine articles, spoke to friends, purchased books on hotel management and did everything I could to learn about what is involved.

We visited the hotel we now own on eight separate occasions before we moved here, and two weeks before the move I spent the day with the then owners to discuss the takeover. I asked as many questions as I could about the day-to-day running of the hotel and at the time came away from the meeting happy that I had satisfied my curiosity and exhausted all the possible problems that might crop up.

What I now realise is that the then owners would have been guarded in their replies as the last thing they would have wanted was to put me off – and understandably so considering they had sold the business to us and were planning their own future.

But why do *you* want to own a hotel?

So I ask the question again: 'Why do you want to own a hotel?' Is it because you are bored with your daily routine, want to be your own boss, just fancy a change, want to move to a different location, think that it would be an easy option, hate what you are doing now, want to live by the seaside?

Or do you know that it is something you have to do, that it's something you have always wanted to do but never been brave enough to take the plunge?

Examine your reasons, question them. Speak to other people you know. Speak to people who already run their own business. Look at the bad points and the reasons not to do it and see if these outweigh the plus points. Most of all make a decision based on business reasons, not just on emotion. Look at your background and consider which of your work and life experiences are relevant to your future in hotel ownership.

Choosing the hotel that is right for you

This is all important – it will affect how you run the hotel and how you run your life when you start. It is intrinsically linked to the lifestyle you choose and how you finance the purchase. It will also determine your working hours, how many staff you will need, how much holiday you take and of course where you live.

Living separately from the hotel

Although we chose a hotel based mainly on location – location is key as it will determine occupancy levels – when we started to look at possible sites we were primarily looking for a property that had separate living accommodation. We have two small children and we didn't want them to be exposed to guests, and most importantly we didn't want guests to be bothered by children and the noise that this involves. We were also looking for a property that could sustain trade all year round.

There are very few hotels on the market that offer a separate house as the owners' accommodation. In two years of searching I found only five suitable premises and we viewed just three of these. The other two had already been sold before we could arrange a viewing.

Financially, buying a hotel with a separate house will be much more expensive and it is difficult to find a property that is ideal. If you decide to buy this type of business you need to be aware that your living costs will also increase – you will have two bills for all utilities, rates, etc. and you will have two properties to maintain. For us this works well: we have a two-bedroom house on the same plot of land to one side of the hotel. The hotel is a 30-second walk across a courtyard. We can switch the hotel telephone, front-door intercom and reception intercom over to the house telephone when we are not on-site. These are all details that you will need to think about before making a commitment.

Living in the hotel

Living in the hotel has its up and downsides. Generally hotels of this type use rooms for your accommodation which otherwise would be utilised for guest bedrooms or common areas. There will be a separate suite in the basement or on the ground floor or in the attic. Some will have a separate entrance and some will have access via a door off the reception area or one of the other rooms used by guests.

What you need to consider more than anything is how this will affect your privacy. You will always be on-site and at the beck and call of your guests. Once they know that you are on the premises they will not hesitate to call on you for the slightest reason. You only have to walk down the hall after all! You also need to consider what effect this will have on your guests – will they feel awkward if they open the wrong door or find you in your pyjamas enjoying a late night cup of cocoa? On the upside you will have immediate access to your hotel and will know exactly what is happening in your hotel at any time. You will not have to keep guests waiting if they need to talk to you and you will not have to leave the comfort of your living room to walk across from your house in the rain on a dark wet evening in December.

Checking out the location

Knowing as much as you can about the location you are looking at will help you deicide if the hotel matches your chosen lifestyle. If your hotel is in or near to a town centre, close to a business park, near an airport, by the sea, out in the countryside – these factors all have a major bearing on the type of customers you will attract.

It is important to note that we knew all about the hotel's location before we committed to buying. Combined with the trading figures and the then owners' account of life in the area we were able to make an informed decision. You must do the same if you are to run a successful business.

The importance of location

Location really does play a major part. Our hotel is in a busy high street close to several restaurants and public houses. We are surrounded by businesses, local, national and international. We have four business parks of varying sizes within a five minute drive, some within a two-minute walk. We are just 4.5 miles from the M4 and 30 minutes from Bristol and Bath town centres. We have a local train station five-minutes drive away. We have a shopping centre close by and the local police and fire stations are just two minutes away. Bristol airport is a 40-minute drive but far enough away not to create any air pollution.

In addition we have Badminton and Cheltenham within striking distance and these help to attract visitors attending the horse trials and race meetings.

We are on the edge of the Cotswolds and the local area has many attractions. We are just 40 minutes from the seaside and Wales is just 35 minutes across the Severn Bridge. The town has several churches and a town hall, all hosting events including weddings, funerals and christenings.

Financial considerations

Undoubtedly your choice will be influenced by the amount of capital you have to invest and the purchase price of your 'dream' property. Do not make an emotive decision or one just based on your gut instinct or your determination to turn a failing business into a success. There will be a reason why a hotel is not bringing in customers and it is doubtful this will just be the lack of experience of the current owners or their poor management.

You will be given a variety of reasons why the owners are looking to sell and you need to learn to read between the lines. The key pointers are occupancy and turnover. If you have these two indicators you will have 90% of the information you need to make a decision.

Learning our lessons

When we met hotel owners on viewings we learned many valuable lessons. Ask as many questions as you can and prepare before you go. You will find out more by doing so than you can learn from the estate agent's brochure or the hotel's own website.

The importance of viewing

The first hotel that we visited matched our criteria. It had ten guest bedrooms, a bar, a restaurant, a decent size garden and the owners' three-bedroom house was attached to the hotel but had a separate entrance. When we received information on the property it did not mention financial details or occupancy levels. The location too was a possible issue. However, the overall data merited a visit.

The experience of visiting a possible new venture was very exciting and proved to be a valuable exercise. We discovered that the location of the hotel affected trade more than any other factor. The hotel was situated in a village just five miles from a major holiday route into Devon, an 'A' road which featured directional signs from a junction to the hotel. The village was fairly small and had just one other public house. In an effort to increase trade the owners had opened their bar and restaurant to the public.

While the hotel met our requirements in every other way, we soon realised that the owners were struggling to make ends meet. This became apparent on being furnished with their balance sheet, which had not been offered to us ahead of our visit. On future visits we insisted on having access to the financial performance before making an appointment. This will tell you more than anything else whether there are any underlying problems and will save you time.

Some hoteliers choose not to work at weekends, some take holidays and leave their business in the hands of a friend or a temporary manager, and many open all of the time.

Small hotels that open their bar and restaurant to non-residents and host conferences and weddings and other events do so to improve their turnover in many cases because their occupancy levels are too low or they are unable to charge a sufficient tariff to make ends meet. It is doubtful that they work this hard because they enjoy doing so!

Why we chose our hotel

We chose our hotel because it ticked all of our boxes. It is open all year round, with the exception of a week at Christmas, and it already had excellent occupancy levels and an improving turnover.

On a personal level, the area has good schools that score highly with Ofsted, it is close to hundreds of attractions and is within easy reach of the seaside. The town is medieval and in a conservation area and there is a strong community feeling more akin to a village than a town. Everything is on our doorstep – shops, local amenities, the countryside – and we are close to two thriving towns.

Primarily we are a business hotel, with almost 100% occupancy Monday to Thursday. Our opportunity to improve lay in our ability to attract more weekend trade. The previous owners stayed closed on many weekends. We know of some hotels that will only take bookings if customers book for two nights at the weekend – some even do this during the week.

Buying a seaside hotel

If you are considering a seaside hotel then the financial implications are paramount. Equally, if your budget dictates that you need premises that incorporate your living accommodation you must consider how this will affect your day-to-day life.

Many hotels in coastal locations are seasonal. We couldn't afford to work for just four or five months of the year and I didn't want to have to find another job to supplement our income.

If you chose the seaside and are happy to have just a few guests for several months of the year you need to consider if this is financially viable. You might be happy to supplement your income with a second job. You will need to look at how you occupy yourself when the hotel is empty. You will also need to maintain the building to keep it habitable for when guests appear unexpectedly during the winter months, unless of course you decide to close down altogether.

A seasonal seaside property

I came across a hotel that closes for the winter months but is full from late April to October. It has 30 staff! All personnel are retained during closure and therefore receive a salary. The owners are considering opening their restaurant all year to improve turnover. However, they are successful because of their location.

Some seaside resorts are popular all year round. However, this will require you to be open every day and you will have to consider the type of guests that you will entertain, including holidaymakers, hen and stag parties, political party conference delegates and students.

Buying a city-centre hotel

If you decide upon a city-centre hotel you also need to consider whether this is right for you. You need to look at the immediate surroundings and visit the hotel at different times of the week. This will give you an indication of what to expect in the evenings or at weekends and will help you to understand if traffic is a problem. You need to consider whether parking is an issue, not just for you but also for your guests. Even if the hotel has a car park your guests may for some reason have to park in the street. Noise pollution is also a major factor. If the hotel is on a busy road you must find out if it is busy at night or early morning. Are there pubs or nightclubs nearby? Are there particular nights of the week that can be a problem?

Our hotel

Our hotel is on a main high street and while we have a car park it only has room for eight cars. Friday and Saturday evenings are busy with locals visiting the seven public houses and five restaurants. It can be very noisy from midnight to 2 a.m. You need to be prepared to advise guests of what to expect as they will sometimes ask for a quiet room and they will not thank you if you place them on the ground floor facing the road.

Sometimes our guests have to park on the street. We are lucky as there are very few parking restrictions. Again giving sound advice on this is important.

The upside to owning a town centre property is that everything is in close proximity. Guests can walk to the pub or restaurant and taxis are easy to come by. Shops, bus stops and tourist information are all readily available.

Attracting tourism or weekend travellers can prove to be a challenge depending on the location, so look into what is available locally, what attractions are close by and where the nearest bus and train stations are situated. All of this will help you to help your potential customers.

Buying a hotel in the country

You may decide you would like to own a hotel in the country. Business will rely almost exclusively on tourism, weekend guests or events. You may also be involved in offering other facilities such as special weekend packages, pampering weekends or murder mystery weekends. You may also have to offer a function room or the hotel grounds for conferences or weddings.

You need to look carefully at the location and how the hotel attracts custom. You will also need to offer a full service to customers, which will include an evening meal and having an open bar for most of the day. Depending on the location and what the locality has to offer you may also need to provide evening entertainment or run special events. The more you offer the more likely you are to attract customers. And of course the more staff you will need and the harder you will be working!

Buying a hotel abroad

You may also be considering moving abroad. Running a hotel overseas is an even greater challenge. The same rules apply overseas as they do for the UK on running a hotel in a seaside, country or town location. However, you will have the added complications of language, local customs, local suppliers, staffing and, most importantly, local authorities. You may well find yourself dealing solely with holidaymakers and will have to provide full board, be knowledgeable and offer advice on the locality.

The attraction of being in a warm climate all year round will no doubt be appealing. You will need to consider if this outweighs the difficulties living in a foreign land will undoubtedly bring.

> **Running a hotel abroad**
>
> My sister and her husband own a hotel in Spain, up in the hills in a small village just 40 minutes from Malaga airport. The climate is fantastic and they enjoy warm weather for most of the year. The most difficult aspect for them is how to advertise to potential customers sufficiently to ensure a steady stream of guests throughout the year. The hotel can accommodate 14 guests and has a swimming pool. Guests are picked up from the airport if they haven't hired a car. Six days a week they offer breakfast, lunch and an evening meal. The hotel is reasonably isolated and it is difficult for guests to go out for dinner.
>
> My sister's choice of hotel and country was very much based on lifestyle. She works all summer and is busy all of the time. Her working hours involve late nights and early mornings. Guests are catered for virtually 24 hours a day. Unlike a business hotel they have certain weeks and the odd month where they do not have any guests at all and they use this time to maintain the hotel and to rest or take holidays.

Whatever you decide is right for you, knowing what is in store for you when you take over is essential.

Considering the bricks and mortar

Part of your decision-making process when considering what type of hotel is right for you should include the physical structure of the building and the grounds. This may sound obvious but it is essential that your decision be based on every aspect of the business. The fabric of the building is a major part of this.

Survey

You will no doubt have a survey conducted during the buying process. However, there is no point in making a commitment unless you are satisfied that you can cope with the demands the building will make upon you and your budget.

Age of the property

The age of the property will have a bearing on its state of repair and you will soon be able to make you own mind up as to what needs immediate attention and how much this will cost. We looked at two very similar hotels and both required refurbishment before we would have seriously considered them. We estimated that both would have needed £50,000 of work – this made our decision much simpler.

Maintenance

Maintaining the building is an important factor and you need to look at how you will deal with this over the coming years. You also need to be aware of the upkeep of the grounds, how much effort this will involve and how much it will cost.

You should consider the external structure as well as the internal make up of the building. The vendors will be able to furnish you with information and data on any work carried out, any guarantees still valid, how they maintain the building and what will need your attention in the near and distant future.

Do your own survey!

Be aware though that the sellers are not likely to draw your attention to anything they consider might put you off. So take a look at the roof if you can, look in the attic and basements, inspect the window frames, take a good look at any paintwork, ask to see the boiler and any immersion heaters, walk around the grounds – in short leave no stone unturned. Conduct your own survey!

Our hotel

We now own a Grade II listed building and this in itself throws up many concerns. The hotel opened just four years ago and had undergone a total refurbishment turning it from a dwelling into a ten-bedroom hotel.

What your friends/colleagues will tell you!

With very few exceptions our friends, family and colleagues all thought we were completely mad when we announced we had purchased a hotel. We decided not to tell anyone until we had actually made an offer and had it accepted. We had discussed our plans between ourselves on many occasions but felt it would only be the right time to make an announcement once the deal had been made. On reflection this was a good move as it avoided having to face the same questions and comments we encountered once the news was out:

'Are you mad?'
'It's very hard work.'
'What an earth do you want to do that for?'
'You don't have any experience of running a hotel.'

We heard these sorts of comments from nearly everyone time and time again. I always replied in the same way:

'I can't work any harder than I do now.'
'How hard can it actually be?'
'It can't possibly be more tiring than running events for a living.'

My reasons for a change in career

I had worked for myself for seven years organising corporate events on behalf of publishing companies and event organisers. For five months of the year I had worked for seven days a week for up to 90 hours, sometimes more. For the other seven months I worked six days a week. We hardly had time for a holiday.

I had grown weary and was looking for a fresh challenge. I had become dissatisfied with my lot and, looking to the future, I just couldn't see myself running events for other people for the next twenty years. I had grown tired of dealing with incompetent people who tried to tell me how to do my job without any practical experience themselves. I prided myself on being the best event organiser in the business and had an acute eye for detail. I always feel that if you are going to do a job you might as well do it properly. Above all else I was successful and felt my skills could be applied to hotel management.

Unless you are speaking to someone who has actually run a hotel there is little point in taking the comments you receive to heart. They are, however, seriously worth considering and investigating.

Our friends and family were right in the end. It *is* hard work – extremely hard in fact – and nothing can quite prepare you for what is in store. But don't be put off by what people say to you. If you know that you want to change direction and are considering or have already decided that hotel ownership is for you, then go for it! What have you got to lose?

Indeed, once our family and friends knew that we were serious they rallied round in support. We even found many of them had harboured similar ambitions!

Starting with the practicalities

Once you have examined why you want to run a hotel, considered how your lives will change and made your decision on the type of property and location you are interested in, you will find it very liberating! You will then be free to start making appointments to view properties and look at how to finance the deal (see in detail Chapter 3).

Selling your own property

At this stage you also need to be looking at more practical issues. You will need to sell your own property, or at least start to look at how and when you will do this. We placed our house on the market as soon as we had an offer excepted on the hotel. It took four months to sell our house, which felt like an eternity. Our main concern was whether the hotel owners would have the patience to wait for us or if another buyer became interested. We kept in touch with the agency selling the hotel and with the hotel owners, and gave regular updates on our progress. This helped to reassure us and gave us more of an insight into what was happening at the other end of the chain.

Researching your chosen area

We researched our new town and the surrounding areas thoroughly.

We visited the hotel on several occasions. We also spent time in the town and toured the local area. This rubber-stamped our decision. Uprooting your entire life and family is a major step and not one to be taken lightly. Do everything you can to make this easier for yourselves. Spending a few days visiting your new environment and exploring the facilities such as local shops, supermarkets, shopping centres, dentists, doctors, hospitals, cinemas, pubs, restaurants, schools and local attractions will make you feel more at home when you eventually arrive.

Involving the children

If you have children take them with you and include time visiting an attraction that they will enjoy. This puts them at ease at a time when they will be every bit as anxious as you. We took our two boys to visit all of the hotels that we viewed. Although they are very young our oldest son who was five at the time picked up on details that even we missed. Thankfully he liked the hotel we purchased and was excited. Involving him at every stage and discussing this with him eased our decision and made it more acceptable to the children.

We also investigated several of the local schools and visited the two that were within walking distance of the hotel. Both were more than suitable and made us welcome. Thankfully we were offered our first choice.

Checking out the competition

Staying in your closest competitor's hotel without telling them who you are is a valuable exercise. Spending the night in the very place you will live in has many benefits. You will be able to try out the local public houses and a restaurant. You will get a feel for your new town at night and first thing in the morning. You will also pick up tips on how to run your hotel and you will learn what your competitor offers to guests.

Checking out the details

You will no doubt have stayed in other hotels in your lifetime but it is doubtful you will have noticed very much, especially if you were on business. On holiday you are in a different frame of mind and you only really notice your environment when something goes wrong.

Staying in a hotel when you own one is a completely different experience and you can learn so much. On your visit you will notice how you are greeted on arrival, the registration form, your host's instructions, your host's appearance, the room key, the reception area, the smells and sounds, and the facilities available to guests.

You will notice the layout of your room, the bed, the bathroom, the TV, the courtesy tray, the carpet and the guests' welcome pack. Once you own your hotel you will notice much more – security and warning notices, fire extinguishers, fire exits, the bedspread, the towels, the soap, the level of cleanliness, the menu, the dining room tables, the chairs – and so it will go on.

Noticing every detail will help you. As a guest you will have your basic requirements and standards and as long as these are met you are relatively happy. Staying in a rival hotel will give you an understanding of what you really need to make a guest's stay comfortable.

After staying in another hotel you will realise that comfort and cleanliness are of paramount importance. It will open your eyes to the mistakes other owners make and it will offer you a guide on how to operate your own hotel.

Qualifications – what you must have!

Personal licence

You will need to begin to look at the qualifications you must have to become a hotelier. If your hotel has a bar or if you will be running events with alcohol supplied you will need to become a *personal licence holder*. If you are a couple running the business at least one of you will have to take a course and pass an examination. The internet will provide you with several choices of training companies providing courses.

The course, usually run over one day, involves a multiple-choice examination at the end of the day. The exam is in two parts and you must answer all of the questions in the first part correctly if you are to obtain a pass. The course is interesting and designed to help you pass the exam. Once you have passed you will be issued with a BIIAB Level 2 National Certificate for Personal Licence Holders.

Once in possession of your certificate you will have to provide evidence that you do not have a criminal record. 'Disclosure Scotland' will issue you with a basic disclosure, which details any convictions, reprimands, warnings or cautions. Additionally, you must also provide the consent of the existing premises licence holder to transfer the premises licence to you.

The local licensing authority will issue you with a 'Notice of Grant of an Application for the Variation of a Designated Premises Supervisor' under the Licensing Act 2003. This must be issued to take effect from the day you take over.

Once you have all of this information your application must be submitted to the local authority covering the location of your hotel. I visited the local council offices dealing with personal licences two weeks before we moved and they issued the relevant documents while I waited.

Once issued the licence is valid for a period of ten years. The licence may on application be renewed for a further ten years. Your renewal application must be made before the expiry of the existing licence.

A personal licence holder may only hold one personal licence at any time and the licence is valid in England and Wales regardless of where it is issued. As a holder of a personal licence you must comply with the statutory requirements of the Licensing Act 2003. The Act is based on four key objectives: the prevention of crime and disorder, public safety, the prevention of public nuisance and the protection of children from harm.

You will undoubtedly lose your licence if you break the law. You must consider how this would affect your ability to run the business.

Foundation Certificate in Food Hygiene

The Foundation Certificate in Food Hygiene involves a day-long course with a multiple-choice examination at the end of the day. The exam also contains a section in which you must answer all questions correctly if you are to achieve a pass. Once you have taken and passed the course you will be issued with a certificate which should be displayed in the kitchen of your hotel. A refresher course every three years is advisable.

The course itself is interesting and instructive and has helped me to run the hotel more effectively. It covers all aspects of food safety and hygiene and will ensure that you work safely and within government legislation. The examination is fairly straightforward as long as you pay attention. The course is designed to ensure that you obtain a pass and all of the exam questions are covered more than once during the day.

It is recommended that if you are a couple running a hotel you should both attend the course. If you have kitchen staff it is advisable, if the budget permits, for you to arrange their attendance at a course. You will find that the content also helps you in other areas of the hotel, not just the kitchen. If you take what you learn into the day-to-day management of your hotel and apply your new-found knowledge you will find that your hotel runs more efficiently and is a cleaner and safer environment for all concerned.

Personally I have followed what I learned to the letter, particularly in the hotel kitchen. It has helped me to install daily procedures which ensure that the kitchen is always clean and is a safe place to work. I spend between three and four hours a day in the kitchen so it is also important that you enjoy the environment.

Premises licence

This is issued by the local council's licensing authority and covers the times the licence authorises licensable activities, i.e. the opening times of your bar if you have one and the times you may serve alcohol. It also covers the opening hours of your premises and the licensable activities allowed, such as the sale by retail of alcohol, recorded music and late night refreshment.

The licence summary must be displayed in a prominent position within the hotel. The hotel will no doubt already have a premises licence and as such you should apply to have this transferred to yourselves and the licensing authority will issue you with a 'Notice of Grant of Transfer'. Again this must be issued to take effect from the day you take over.

Other licences

You will also need a TV licence and the fee is calculated on the number of units of overnight accommodation you have to let with television receiving equipment in them. One full fee covers the first 15 units of accommodation. If you live in the hotel or live in a separate house within the grounds of the hotel the licence will cover the TV set in your home as well. The fee in 2007 based on 1–15 units is £135.50; 16–20 units cost £271.00. Full details can be obtained from the TV Licensing Authority – their website is at www.tvlicensing.co.uk.

A PRS (Performing Rights Society) licence allows you lawfully to play music in your business. The licence covers any music your guests may hear during their stay with you that is played by you on a radio, CD, DVD, TV or any other recording equipment. The PRS ensures that composers, songwriters and music publishers receive payment whenever their music is performed in public. The licence for 2007 cost £115.42 including VAT. Full details can be found at www.prs.co.uk/musiclicense.

2
Being your own boss – the reality

Why is being your own boss so appealing?

Not having to answer to anyone else, no boss or supervisor or manager or director to tell you what to do or to moan at you if you are late for work – sounds ideal, doesn't it? Well in most respects it is – in fact it is heaven. Even if you have run your own business before or worked from home, you will most probably have had to work for a client or customer.

In a hotel you will still have customers and they pose a different set of problems. However, they are not in charge – you are. They will rely on you to look after them and they will have demands. The difference is that they will be with you for a relatively short space of time and when they have departed you may never set eyes on them again! Ideally of course they will be back time and time again.

Not having to consult anyone else on decisions to be made, other than each other, is also a major plus point to running a hotel. Be warned, however, that this can also be difficult, as you may not have anyone else to give you advice or to tell you how to overcome a particular problem. I do sometimes find this daunting but at the same time it is challenging. Thinking through a problem before taking action and then solving it can be very rewarding.

Problem-solving on the hoof!
Our gas cooker recently developed a fault. The element in the grill stopped working. No warning given, it just stopped during breakfast one morning. We were cooking bacon and had several guests yet to come down for breakfast. We continued with breakfast

and started to fry the bacon instead of using the grill. The point is that I had nobody to ask what to do except my waitress. The guests didn't notice a difference other than perhaps the taste of the bacon. Not panicking and finding a different cooking method solved the problem almost instantly.

After breakfast I had to decide what to do next. Our gas service provider doesn't cover the grill section of the cooker as this part is electric. I consulted with the previous owners' records and found that the problem had arisen before. They had made a note of the details of the company who supplied the spare part. I called the supplier and ordered a replacement. Within a few days my electrician had fitted the part and the cooker was back to normal.

Everyday stuff really, but an example of something that is likely to happen to you at some stage. These types of problems crop up all of the time and it is always your responsibility to find a solution. Not letting these problems upset you and looking upon them as a challenge that can be overcome with logical thinking will ensure that you enjoy your new-found freedom.

Making the most of your staff

You may also have staff working for you. We have several part-time staff. You may decide to do everything yourselves but I doubt you will have the time to do so. Your staff offer you the opportunity to discuss and solve problems and to find more efficient ways of working. We try to involve our staff as much as we can in day-to-day issues. This can help share the burden of decision-making. More importantly, they may well know more than you do and are able to offer a solution. Equally it makes your staff feel involved with the business and this can only be a positive thing.

As the 'boss' all decisions are yours to make. Right or wrong they are yours and yours alone. If you make the wrong decision you have nobody to answer to. There may well be repercussions but again, as the boss, you will be in charge of making good.

Are you the right type of person/people to run a hotel?

You need to examine your background and look at your previous experience. Even if on the face of it this doesn't appear to offer you guidance, you will find that there is always something that will be relevant.

You must like people and be happy to look after them. You need to enjoy working with your staff. When guests stay in your hotel it is your responsibility to ensure that they enjoy the experience. If you don't like people then you will find the job very challenging.

Looking after your guests

When people stay in a hotel they know that someone else is cleaning up after them and so the majority of guests pay little attention to being tidy. You can't let this type of behaviour upset you.

You must be self-motivated and prepared to work long hours. I am up at 5.54 a.m. every weekday and at 6.54 a.m. on the weekends. You simply cannot afford to oversleep when you have 20 breakfasts to prepare. Your guests rely on you and expect high standards.

Going the extra mile

You must be willing to go the extra mile for customers. Having stayed in many of the UK's top hotels on business I appreciate how annoying it can be when you do not feel you are receiving a good service or when the front-of-house personnel obviously have little regard for you as a customer. With a small hotel you have to be on your best form all of the time. Equally you must be willing to help your guests when they ask you for something or request information, and you must deliver this promptly and with a smile on your face.

Encouraging your staff to look after your guests

Your staff should be encouraged to adopt the same attitude. When we took over our hotel we were surprised to find that the staff had been discouraged from speaking to guests. We actively encourage them to pass the time of day with our customers and to be polite and helpful. We often receive comments from customers about our staff. This is something guests will remember when they are looking for accommodation in the future. It is part of the mix of running a successful business.

Fixing problems yourself

You will become a jack-of-all-trades. Everyday something different happens which will require a different skill. This can be anything from a malfunctioning vacuum cleaner to a blown light bulb. You may have a blocked sink in a bedroom or a stain on a carpet or a broken window. The list is seemingly endless.

We have several local tradesmen that we can call upon. However, this can prove to be expensive and in many instances you will have to fix the problem yourselves. If this is something you are not already familiar with or used to, you will need to adapt or find ways to work through these problems. Keeping on top of any problems that arise and dealing with them straightaway will give you peace of mind and ensure the hotel operates efficiently.

How much fun/hard work is it really?

In my previous job I worked between 12 and 20 hours a day, every day. A normal working week for me was 80–90 hours and this continued for months on end. The difference now is that we work for ourselves so any profit (or loss) is ours.

It *is* hard work. All of our friends who warned us that running a hotel is hard work were spot on. They of course had no idea really. Unless you have run your own hotel you will never know what is involved. Every day is different. Many of the daily routines are the same but when you are dealing with people anything can happen.

You are always on call and the hotel does take over your life. You have to consider the hotel before you do anything else. You have to look at what will happen to the hotel if you are not there. The only time you are not thinking about the hotel is when you are asleep!

Our new life

I first started to consider what life would be like when we took over the hotel about a week before we moved. Sounds ridiculous, but we were so taken up with all the arrangements that we didn't really have time to think about ourselves. I can remember thinking that our lives would change completely: we would always be responsible for our guests and for the hotel – a daunting feeling and one that filled me with doubt.

Meeting people

Meeting different people every day and facing new challenges is good fun. Even miserable guests or people that are rude are interesting.

I deal with these types of people by trying to imagine why they have become like this, what has happened to them to make them behave in this manner. If we have a regular guest who is always rude or miserable I will always treat them the same, with respect and politeness. I try to win them over by always being courteous. This does work and eventually they will come round. There is a fine line to be trod and sometimes people just don't want to speak to you, for whatever reason. We have encountered many people like this and the trick is to recognise when they want to be left alone. Quite often a good night's sleep, a hearty breakfast and some peace and quiet is all that they need.

When I get upset . . .

I have an imaginary think bubble above my head and, if a guest upsets me, my thoughts enter the bubble and stay there. They never reach the customer and I feel content with keeping my thoughts to myself. Again you can have a lot of fun this way and nobody gets hurt!

Looking back

I also think back to what life was like before – long hours, mostly sat in front of a computer, hundreds of enquiries every day, mostly from people who could have worked the answer out for themselves if only they had tried. I never did settle into corporate life and couldn't play the game that most of my colleagues revelled in. I found it all too false and didn't want to crawl and squirm my way to the top. It just isn't in me. I prefer an honest and straightforward approach and this really helps when dealing with guests and enquiries. I always answer the telephone professionally. However, I do try to have fun with the person on the other end of the line, especially if they are making a booking enquiry.

Having some fun with the customers

I once took an early morning call while preparing breakfast. The voice on the other end of the line asked me for my reservations. I replied by saying that I was worried about the weather report, that I didn't like the winter months and that I hoped business would be good over the Christmas period. My staff all looked at me with puzzlement and thought I had finally flipped. The caller just laughed and it really broke the ice and she booked straightaway.

On another call a lady asked for our prices, as she couldn't find them on our website. I replied by saying that we didn't advertise our prices as we are really expensive and we didn't want to put people off! Sounds a bit Basil Faultyish but the caller loved the reply. She had called hotels all over Bath but couldn't get a room. She was planning a family night out and although we were 30 minutes from Bath and not particularly convenient to her plans she booked with us during the call.

Of course you can be like this with guests when you own the hotel. You can usually tell when somebody is not susceptible to a laugh and a joke and it is important not to be rude, but there is no rule that I know of that prohibits having fun in this way.

My journey into work every day is a short 30-second walk across a courtyard. I don't have to sit on a train or bus or tube anymore, or spend an hour and a half in a car fighting the London traffic. When guests are checking out each morning I often ask them if they have a busy day ahead. I already know that they do as they are away from home for a purpose and it will always involve

25

travel and dealing with people they probably don't like very much. This to me is fun. I don't have to do what they are doing anymore. I did for 20 odd years and by the end I was extremely tired of travel and sitting in an office everyday.

Making money

Making money is fun too. Of course it is. We spend any profit we make on the hotel and trying to improve our guests' experience. It is an investment in our future. Making the hotel a popular place and a success financially is also fun. It is important to remember to have fun and to enjoy life in a hotel. It can of course be stressful and it can be annoying when things don't always go your way but it is important to make the most of every situation and try to turn problems into opportunities.

Following my dream

My father-in-law once asked me if I had considered what would happen to us if we went bankrupt. He was of course concerned about the family unit and in particular what would happen to his daughter and grandsons. I am not sure he liked my reply very much. I am following my dream. The alternative was to continue with my business organising events and gradually become more miserable. If we did go bankrupt I would at least have had a go at something different and wouldn't get to the end of my working life regretting that I hadn't been more adventurous.

It's not all fun . . .

On the whole life is much harder than it once was, in many ways. The pressure of constantly being available and of running your own business can be exhausting, if you let it.

Starting work each day at 6.30 a.m. was foreign to me to begin with. Although I had previously worked long hours I never started before 9 a.m. and didn't mind working late. You do get used to early mornings eventually. Winter is the hardest time. I found the first winter exceptionally difficult. Getting out of bed at 5.54 a.m. in the dark and the day not becoming light until after 7.30 a.m. was one of the hardest things I have had to get through. We are now into our second winter and it is not nearly so difficult. You become accustomed to a new way of life and your body and mind compensate.

Our new life

Depending on where you live in the country, if you move to a totally new area you will also have to become accustomed to your new environment. You need to consider this and how it will affect you, though it didn't become apparent to us before we moved. We were based near London and we moved to the Westcountry. Everything is different – the climate, the sky, the people, the pace of life – it is almost as if we had moved to another country altogether. It stays light here until later in the evening during the winter – only 10 or 15 minutes but enough to make a difference. It also stays darker for longer in the mornings and some days it doesn't become completely light until 8 a.m.

We now live in a small town where the sights and sounds are different. The hotel is situated on a main road which is quiet at night but busy during the day. At weekends the street is very noisy and to begin with this kept us awake.

We also live at the top of a hill and are just 40 minutes from the sea. We can now tell what the weather will be like later in the day as we can see it coming in off the sea. The sky seems much bigger here. Winters are harsher and we have more rain and wind.

Your new environment will make a difference to how you feel about your new life and how happy you will be. You do become acclimatised but it takes time, so be patient and try to enjoy this new experience.

What qualifications do I need to run a hotel?

Apart from the personal licence and Food Hygiene Certificate mentioned in Chapter 1 you don't need to be qualified in anything particular. You may consider basic qualifications that will help you practically such as first aid or health and safety but academically the key requirement is nothing more than common sense and a sense of humour.

If you have marketing or sales experience this will definitely help. You may also consider basic book-keeping.

I didn't really know why I wanted to run a hotel. It just appealed to me. When I investigated my family tree I found that several of my ancestors had been involved in the hotel industry. You might find the same. However, you do need to look at how your existing experience and qualifications can be used to good effect, how these will benefit the business and how they can save you money.

How running a hotel will affect you and your way of life

Consider how your life is now. Look at all aspects of your daily routine.

◆ What do you do at weekends?

◆ What do you enjoy doing in the evenings?

◆ Where do you go on holiday?

◆ How often do you have days off?

◆ How much spare time do you have each day?

◆ What do you do together or as a family?

All of this will change – your new life will be unrecognisable in comparison to your old way of life.

For the first couple of years everything will be different. You will not have time to do the same things or continue with your hobbies or interests. You have to put all of your energy into your business. Forget having weekends off or going on holiday. Unless you are buying a hotel and do not need a mortgage and haven't invested all of your money into the business, you will not have time to continue with your existing lifestyle. That is presumably why you want to try something new.

How others manage

We do know and have met several other hotel owners. Some continue to take holidays and have weekends off. It can be done, but not all of the time, and it takes money and a consistently high occupancy level to do this.

We also know of people that have taken over a hotel and work harder than we do. They have a relatively low occupancy level but are a very successful weddings and functions venue. Yet after just a year in the business they are looking to sell up and find a less demanding hotel – one that doesn't have to rely on events to make ends meet.

We know other hotel owners where one of the partners has a day job and the other runs the hotel. They enjoy the business but they also only open when they need to. They have many weekends off and if the weekdays are busy they don't need to rely on the income from weekend trade.

You need to research the area you plan to move to and seriously consider the type of business you would like to run.

Knowing your strengths and weaknesses

You also need to recognise your strengths and weaknesses and analyse how these will be of use to you and how they can be applied to running a hotel.

We chose to run a small ten-bedroom hotel in a busy location because we recognised that as novices we had to learn the trade before we could consider anything on a grander scale. We also recognise that our success in running this type of hotel lies in high occupancy levels. We have dabbled in running small events and have considered opening as a restaurant and providing evening meals. After just a year we know what we are capable of and what the hotel can withstand. We firmly believe that this is the key to running a small hotel.

3
The purchase – practical advice on the initial stages

Location, location, location

If, like us, your budget is tight from the outset then location will be the single most important element and you must investigate and research your chosen location thoroughly.

Avoid making emotive decisions based on your dream location alone. You may have decided to live by the sea or in the countryside and have found 'on paper' what appears to be your dream hotel. Whatever you do, investigate as much as you can about the place before you even make a visit. You must look at every aspect of the location of the hotel – not just its location in the country but its position locally, where it is in relation to major roads, where it is placed in the county, the nearby towns and villages, its proximity to other similar hotels and guest houses.

If the owners claim that their occupancy during the week is derived either solely or mostly from business customers, then you should look at why the customers choose to stay there.

◆ Is it easily accessible from major trunk roads?

◆ Is it close to a railway or bus station?

◆ Does it have a car park?

◆ Is it close to a business park?

◆ Are there restaurants and pubs close by?

If the hotel is in a seaside destination you must find out when the season starts and finishes. You should find out if the hotel attracts other types of clientele and the occupancy levels for out of season. You should also look at where the hotel is situated and in particular at its main competitors. Additionally, you should investigate the visitor figures and demographics for the town, the county and the region. These will tell you whether the area is popular and – more importantly – why it is popular.

> We looked at the tourist information figures available online and we looked at the position of the town within the Cotswolds. We also talked at length with the owners and asked questions about the types of people they attracted at weekends. This told us that our location is not a place that attracts holiday trade but is more of a day-trippers' destination. It also gave us an insight into the types of people that lived in the region and their social status. This allowed us to plan how we would increase occupancy at times when historically the hotel had been relatively quiet. It also enabled us to plan our marketing.

Assessing our location

We feel that we have found what must be a near perfect location for the type of hotel we run. The town is located on the edge of the Cotswold escarpment. However, it is not considered to be part of the Cotswolds by the Cotswold Tourist Information Board. They do not cover our town in their marketing or on their website. We applied to advertise with them and were informed that we could not as we were in the Bristol area and as such were covered by a different tourist information service. Although we were disappointed to begin with, it is now apparent that the town is just not the type of place people chose for a week or two's holiday.

We are based in a main high street, only 4.5 miles from the M4 and 13 miles from the M5. We have a train station a five-minute drive away and Bristol and Bath are 30 minutes away. The town itself boasts many local and national companies and the adjoining town features several business parks. If you drive into the next town, which is just a couple of minutes away, the main road is home to around 20 businesses including a division of the council for the county. All of these businesses are our customers.

The seaside is 40 minutes away and Chepstow in Wales takes 25 minutes. Cardiff is around an hour away. We are en route to Devon and Cornwall and we attract visitors from the East and North of the country who stop over for a break before a holiday in the Westcountry.

Because we are close to the M4 we are in easy reach of London and Heathrow. Bristol airport is 45 minutes from here, and many of the local businesses receive visits from international colleagues and customers so we are ideally situated. Once their visitors arrive they do not have to be up early in the morning to ensure they arrive for a meeting on time.

The town has a high percentage of senior citizens, and many have relatives or friends living in other parts of the country. These relatives often visit and need somewhere to stay.

We have several churches within walking distance and the local registry office is just a five-minute drive. The town hall is across the road and plays host to wedding receptions and a variety of other events and functions. There are several golf courses close by with the nearest just a five-minute drive away (in a car!). This supplies a constant flow of potential customers to the town and much of our marketing is geared towards targeting the local population.

Looking at the downside

The only downside, if you can call it this, is that we are always busy. We have very little spare time and absolutely no time for holidays. In your first year it will not necessarily be apparent what the trends are month on month for occupancy, even if the previous owners have left you with their records. Moreover, if you become more successful than they were your occupancy will change.

Our hotel before we started was busy during the week, though much less so at the weekend. It wasn't until we had run the hotel for several months that we realised the reasons for this so we could target an increase in weekend trade. This was key to improving on the already impressive turnover.

Summing up

Location, if you have all the other ingredients of a successful hotel, will almost certainly dictate how busy you are and how hard you have to work.

Financing your purchase – how much will it all cost?

Knowing how much it will cost you to buy a hotel as well as sell your own home and possibly your existing business would on paper appear to be straightforward. Surely there is a formula for working this out and your bank or building society would definitely be able to tell you, wouldn't they?

Looking back at our experience

In our experience this was one of the most difficult parts of preparing for making the purchase. We knew how much the hotel was on the market for and made an offer before we found out whether we could afford the purchase. So convinced were we that it was the perfect business for us that we decided to make the offer and then look into obtaining a mortgage. After all, approaching a mortgage lender with just a vague idea of how much we wanted to borrow based on a dream rather than reality just wasn't a viable option.

Even when we had a deal agreed with a lender it wasn't clear exactly how much the final bill would come to. I had to work out all of the possible variables and arrived at an estimate, or rather an educated guess. Surely this isn't a sound basis on which to go into a new business? It was, however, our only option. Everybody we spoke to that we imagined would have been in a position to help us either didn't have the formula or didn't want to stick their necks out.

I wanted answers to all sorts of questions.

- How much would stamp duty be?
- What would the solicitors' costs be?
- Would the lender charge an arrangement fee?
- How much would the estate agent charge?
- How much would insurance cost?
- How much would the survey cost?
- What about valuation charges?
- Would we have to pay for searches and Land Registry fees?

And the list goes on.

Budgeting and costing

For us it was more a case of preparing a budget to the best of our abilities, adding in the costs that we knew about and estimating the costs that we knew we would incur and then allowing for the unexpected. Below are details of all the costs we incurred which you might expect. Remember it is prudent to have a contingency fund for the unexpected fees. When you have come up with your estimate for this my advice is to double it!

Costs of purchase and set up

- Hotel purchase cost
- Separate living accommodation/house purchase cost
- Stamp duty on hotel purchase
- Stamp duty on private property sale
- Solicitors' fees on own private property sale
- Solicitors' fees on hotel sale
- Survey/valuation
- Mortgage broker arrangement fee
- Mortgage lender arrangement fee
- Fixtures and fittings

◆ Estate agents' fees on own property sale

◆ Pre-contract searches

◆ Land Registry fees

◆ Other searches

◆ Hotel stock and advance payments

◆ Contingency

Other costs

◆ BIIAB course

◆ Hygiene course

◆ First aid course

◆ BHA membership

◆ Council premises and licence fees

◆ Removal costs

◆ Business insurance

Choosing the right finance option – who to turn to and who to avoid

Trying the banks and building societies

Once you have made your decision and you have had an offer accepted, you will then need to arrange finance, unless of course you already have sufficient funds readily available!

When I initially had difficulty finding someone sensible to discuss my requirements I resorted to the internet. I found several so called 'commercial lenders' willing on paper to offer unsecured loans. The interest rate was off the scale. To test the water I filled in an online application. Within a day I received an offer of an £850,000 loan, at 8.5% interest. I had no intention of accepting the offer but at least I had discovered that it was possible to secure the money that we needed.

When I spoke to my own bank and asked for the commercial department I was put through to a very agreeable young lady. She was very excited about my plans and I started to feel that I was heading in the right direction. I had two 40-minute calls with her and she was very supportive, and of course the bank would be delighted to help us. After all I had been a customer with them for just under 30 years. How wrong and misguided could I be? They turned me down on the third call and I realised I had not been speaking to the right person let alone the right bank.

Next stop was the building society. I made an appointment with one of their commercial managers. This resulted in a similar story to the bank and they turned us down flat almost immediately.

Neither organisation had asked for more than a basic outline of our plan and had made a decision based purely on the amount of money we needed to borrow – even though at this stage it wasn't exactly clear how much this actually was!

I then spoke to a friend who runs her own company arranging residential property mortgages and she put me in contact with a bank that she had worked with and who said they were in the commercial market. I managed to get a little further with them and they accepted a little more information but alas the same result – no deal.

In short I was struggling to make any progress and felt quite despondent. I wasn't about to give up though and started to speak to as many contacts as I could. Eventually I spoke to my accountant and he gave me the details of a broker he had approached in respect of a similar project.

Contacting a broker

I spent an hour speaking to the broker and this eventually led to a meeting with a bank and a loan offer. Without the broker's assistance I am sure that we would still be looking for a deal to this day. He gave me the confidence to continue and his encouragement made me realise that my dream could become a reality.

The main difference was that the broker understood the industry. He had brokered many deals for people in a similar position, including himself. He knew the right people to approach, people who didn't waste time and that also had an appreciation of the market, not just the cost of purchasing a hotel but how the hotel business operates, and more importantly how the people who owned them had to operate.

Yes, the broker cost me a 1% arrangement fee, but I feel that it was more than worth it. They introduced me to two different lenders and both offered us deals. Most importantly the broker never made me feel that a deal couldn't be made, even when we had to rearrange at the eleventh hour with an alternative lender, as I describe below.

Had we not needed to borrow quite so much money, it may have been a different story with the other lenders. We had, however, found our dream hotel, and nothing was going to stop us.

Overcoming the obstacles

We had a difficult time during the mortgage negotiations and having already agreed terms with one lender suddenly found that we would have to find a new deal. Our backer, who initially offered to act as security, had a change of heart at the last minute when it came to signing the contract.

Our original lender had agreed excellent terms, including a business bank account with an overdraft. The mortgage was initially on an interest-only basis, which made a significant difference to the monthly repayment amount. They hadn't insisted on us paying an arrangement fee in advance but had added this to the term of the loan. The fee was 1% of the purchase price. It was an excellent deal and one we felt would help us to make a success of the business both in the short and long term.

With the withdrawal of our security we were left to consider our options. Did we pull out and look for a different less expensive hotel or drop the idea altogether? We were so far advanced in our plans that we had to find a new lender straightaway if we were to continue. Our broker came to the rescue.

The new loan was by no means as comprehensive as the first. It didn't include a business account or overdraft but at least it ensured we could continue. It was an interest-only mortgage with monthly payments fixed for the first year. After this period it became a capital and interest repayment loan.

A year sounds a long time but you will find that it flies by. If your hotel is busy most of the time then a year is no time at all. It is important to realise that if you have pulled out all of the stops to secure your loan, and have spent all or most of your savings, you will need at least two years before you begin to make any financial headway. With this in mind you need a lender who is willing to offer you at least one year at interest only, if not two or three.

Looking back

If you require a large sum of money (we borrowed just short of £1m) you will need to speak to the commercial department of a lender who already operates in the hotel industry. These people are not easy to find on your own and it is doubtful that approaching your bank and asking for the commercial department will put you in touch with the right people.

I wasted hours on the telephone talking to my bank and a building society and I realise now that the people I had approached were not ever going to be in a position to help us. It was really frustrating and I began to think that it wasn't going to be possible after all. I was, however determined to succeed and spoke to as many people about the situation as I could.

Writing a business plan – what to include

Unfortunately it isn't as simple as just asking for a loan and being offered whatever you ask for – you do need a business plan. This takes some considerable effort. I spent several weeks writing and rewriting ours. I approached our good friend who runs the mortgage company mentioned above, and she kindly read the plan, made comments and advised us on what was missing. It took several rewrites before I was finally confident that I had produced a document that would secure our future.

There is a skill to writing such a plan. It needs to include sufficient information to prove to your prospective lender that you have done your homework. More than that, it needs to demonstrate that you understand what you are letting yourself in for and that you have researched the hotel industry and the location of your new business thoroughly. Most importantly, it needs to prove that you will be in a position to make the loan repayments.

Before you make a start on your plan you need to consider what you already know about the hotel industry and what you know about buying a property. You also need to think about your own business experience and how this is relevant – if it is relevant – to your planned new career.

Consider who it is that will actually read the plan and what effect it will have on them. Put yourself in their shoes and make a list of all the things you would expect the document to include.

If you have previously written business proposals, take some time to read through them. Note the layout and content and whether you won the business as a result of the plan. If not, what was missing that made the difference?

As we were offered a loan by two different lenders I believe that our business plan included all of the necessary information. Looking back at the plan two years later it is an interesting and valuable exercise to analyse where we are now and how much of our plan was accurate.

Our plan totalled 7,251 words and covered 31 pages. It took several weeks to finalise and I searched for as much relevant data as I could find from a variety of sources. These included:

- the sales information from the seller's estate agent;
- the hotel brochure and website;
- the National Tourist Board;
- the regional tourist information service;
- local newspapers;
- local websites.

Wherever I used data in the plan, I always gave the name of the source to show where the information came from.

Constructing your business plan

Your business plan should include the following content:
- history and background of your chosen hotel;
- the hotel layout;
- the location of the hotel and key data on its locality;
- competitive businesses in the area;
- the trading history of the hotel;
- occupancy rates and local tourism information;
- plans for moving forward with the business;
- the projected income of the hotel;
- a SWOT analysis;
- details about your own background and work history;
- a summary;
- an appendix.

Below are brief notes on the information and data.

History and background of your chosen hotel

- The length of time that the property has been operating as a hotel.
- The background of the current owners and why they are looking to sell.
- The history of the building and its state of repair, internally and externally.

The hotel layout

- A description of the hotel, its grounds and the fabric of the building.
- A description of the layout of the hotel and its internal floor area, including a floor plan if one is available.

The location of the hotel and key data on its locality

◆ This should describe the exact location of the hotel with the distance in miles to nearby towns, villages, major trunk roads and transport links.

◆ If the hotel is based in a town or village you should detail the layout of the place and your position within it. Include brief details of local amenities, places of interest, restaurants and public houses.

◆ You should add any other relevant information which you feel makes the place an attractive destination for potential customers.

◆ If the hotel is rural or coastal you should concentrate on what brings people to the area and the attractions that ensure that it is a popular destination.

◆ Include figures on the local population and the social classes they fall into. These figures are usually available online from local newspapers. Note that these statistics will give you an indication of what to expect in the way of custom drawn from the local population.

◆ You may also include a list of the local newspapers serving the area. These may become useful sources of information to you in the future as they list local tradespeople, carry advertising and give details of forthcoming events.

Competitive businesses in the area

◆ List other hotels, guest houses and bed and breakfast's within a ten-mile radius, with a focus on those closest to you. Include the total number of available hotel bedrooms within your immediate locale.

◆ Detail as much information as you can find on your main competitors and include their addresses, number of rooms, tariffs, function rooms and websites for each. This will become a useful source of reference in the future and will help you to keep in touch with how your competitors operate. Include:

– restaurants, tea rooms, public houses and any other types of business offering similar facilities;

– shops, tourist information offices, banks, post offices and any other type of business that maybe useful to you and your customers;

– other local businesses and any potential or existing sources of trade.

◆ Listing any local major company names is also useful, as it will demonstrate that you have researched this thoroughly. The local company names we listed in our business plan are all now valued customers.

◆ This information also helps you to build a picture of your local community and gives you an indication of how this will assist you in building your business.

The trading history of the hotel

◆ The hotel type, i.e. country, business, tourist, seaside, and how long the hotel has been trading.

◆ How the current owners trade, i.e. focusing on business, weekend or a mixture of both. Also include the background of the owners, how long they have been there and how long they have been in the hotel trade.

Occupancy rates and local tourism information

Our hotel had increased its occupancy levels year on year since opening in 2003. From a modest beginning trade had gradually been built up so that when we took over in June 2006 it had reached 65%. Since May 2007 the hotel has been trading on average at 70% occupancy levels.

This is a clear sign that our influence on the business has had a significant impact but also that the previous owners had provided us with a solid foundation on which to continue trading.

What the figures show

Occupancy levels give you a clear picture of how your hotel is trading and how successful it has been. Including these figures in your plan is essential. The effect is twofold. They demonstrate the success of the business but also give you an indication of how you need to build upon this.

By including occupancy levels you can prove that the business is viable. It also allows you the opportunity to describe your plans to maintain and improve these rates.

National and regional figures

You will need to research national occupancy levels. We sourced our data from the *UK Occupancy Survey for Serviced Accommodation – Annual Report 2004*. The survey was commissioned by the four National Tourist Boards, supported by the then Department for Culture, Media and Sport.

It should be noted that at the time I compiled our figures, the 2004 UK annual average for room occupancy of 61% was higher than it had been in each of the four preceding years.

You also need to include the annual occupancy rate for your region and whether this was affected by any major factors. When working on our business plan the South West had been badly affected by the foot and mouth outbreak.

Value of tourism

In this section of your plan it is also prudent to discuss the value of tourism, especially if this is your hotel's main source of income. This information can be sourced from the region's tourism authority.

This should detail visitor expenditure by type of spend, i.e. food and drink, accommodation, shopping, travel and visitor attractions. It should also include the number of visitors to the region and how many of these visited for a holiday or on business. We sourced this particular information from the UK Tourism Survey (UKTS). This will also give you seasonality of tourism, which is important when you are planning when you will be at your busiest.

Plans for moving forward with the business

This section should detail how the hotel has been operated over the last five years and discuss its successes and failings. It should pinpoint the areas in which the business could and should improve, how you plan to approach this and the length of time you feel you will take to move the business forward.

Your research should, by now, have identified why the location is a perfect position from which to trade, and this should be highlighted as the main opportunity for you, as hoteliers, to improve turnover and raise occupancy levels.

If occupancy is low you need to identify why and discuss how this can be improved. There may well be a very simple explanation. The owners may not have opened all of the time; they may have taken every weekend off or not been very busy out of season. It can depend on why they chose to run a hotel in the first place or if financially they didn't need to open every day.

First-year plan

Include a plan of your first year and list the key points that exhibit how you will operate and how you plan to move the business forward step by step. Then discuss each point in more detail.

Our first-year plan included:
◆ maintaining the existing monthly turnover;
◆ increasing the business customer base;
◆ reviewing room rates;
◆ joining the Chamber of Commerce and other regional business associations;
◆ redesigning the hotel website and brochure;
◆ reviewing the existing marketing campaign;
◆ opening at weekends;
◆ exploring new business opportunities;
◆ reviewing expenditure;

- reviewing staffing levels;
- continuing with existing business.

This information is of value to you in the future once you have started to trade. It is an excellent yardstick and will remind you of the plans that you made and will confirm if you have followed or achieved them. Looking back at our plan, we have either followed or investigated all of the objectives that we set for our first year. We have introduced most of our ideas and been fortunate enough to follow them through to a successful outcome.

This section of your business plan is one of, if not the most, important as it should help you identify whether the business you hope to buy is viable. You should, at this point, be questioning every angle and looking into all possible areas for potential revenue streams. You should be looking closely at the business at it stands currently, how it is trading, what additional revenue streams outside bedroom revenue have been introduced and what you feel is missing from the business. Identifying what is missing and then investigating why this is missing will give you ideas of your own to introduce.

Medium-term plans

You also need to demonstrate that you are thinking beyond the first year and how you will progress the business over the next five years.

If the hotel you plan to buy is already trading at 70%+ occupancy level and has in excess of £200k turnover, future plans will no doubt include how you will maintain this level of business.

Our business plan detailed the following key objectives for the future:
- increase turnover and profitability;
- maintain and improve upon the quality of customer service;
- increase occupancy levels to 75%+;
- increase business client occupancy rate;
- establish the hotel as a tourist hotel at weekends and during the summer months;

◆ establish the business as a venue for weddings and family events;

◆ execute plans for other opportunities identified as viable once operating the hotel.

With the exception of the objective to establish the hotel as a tourist destination, all of the other objectives are more than achievable. We have found, since taking over, that our town is not a main tourist destination. This in the main is attributable to the fact that it is on the edge of the Cotswolds. It is more of a place of interest for afternoon or day visits than a holiday destination.

Long-term plans

You should also include your long-term plans. You may have decided to build a hotel empire and open a chain of hotels bearing your name. You may see the opportunity as a route into early retirement. You will probably have set yourselves a time limit and plan to work in the hotel industry for a five- or ten-year period.

Whatever your reasons, you should be looking to increase turnover thus adding value to your investment. This will only occur if you trade successfully and your plans should detail how you will achieve this.

The projected income of the hotel

A three-year projection should be sufficient. Include the figures for the last two or three years of trading and detail how you plan to improve upon these over the forthcoming two to three years. The existing owners should be happy enough to supply you with their profit and loss account. If you are going to buy the hotel from them this is a must.

Forecast for a gradual increase with a higher percentage increase in your second year. You will be busy establishing yourselves in year 1 and there is little point in forecasting huge increases in turnover straightaway – unless of course the previous owners only opened when it suited them and they have proved to you that the potential is just waiting to be tapped and it is just a matter of staying open all of the time.

Include expenditure for the same length of time. We forecast for a 10% increase in year 1 and 15% in years 2 and 3. You will have a record of the expenditure from the existing owners. However, they will have been running the business as they saw fit and even if you identify where you can make savings it is impossible to be certain if these are viable before you take over. It can be very difficult to forecast for certain expenditure, such as rates and utilities, as these can increase at any time and fluctuate depending on where you are based.

The figures you give should tally with your future plans. You need to show that the increase in turnover will be as a result of the successful implementation of your plans.

A SWOT analysis

SWOT stands for strengths, weaknesses, opportunities and threats. Our lender requested this analysis specifically. If you have worked in sales or run your own business before you will be familiar with this exercise.

Again this is very useful information to look back on. Doing so will enable you to gauge your progress at regular intervals.

Strengths

Under strengths you should include everything that you can think of that reflects positively on the hotel and the business opportunity it represents. You may include:

◆ the location;

◆ the building;

◆ the existing level of business;

◆ the existing customer base;

◆ the potential to expand;
◆ the size of the business and whether it is manageable; the type of trade (seasonal, business, all year round . . .);
◆ the quality of rooms;
◆ the mix of type of rooms (i.e. twin, double, family);
◆ the fixtures and fittings;
◆ the decor;
◆ the reputation;
◆ the trading figures;
◆ any other aspects of the business that make it viable.

Weaknesses

Weaknesses will mainly have resulted from the previous owners' reign. However, you must include this information as it highlights your understanding of the way in which the hotel has been trading. It also pinpoints where you will be able to improve the business. We included in our plan the fact that the hotel had only been trading for three years and was relatively unproven. We added that the hotel had relied mainly on business guests and that the previous owners had had no previous experience of running a hotel.

Opportunities

Under opportunities you must detail the areas that you have identified as being those that can be improved upon. These may include:
◆ the potential to open during previously quiet periods;
◆ improvement in occupancy of business guests;
◆ the potential to add new areas of the business;
◆ the potential to improve the reputation of the hotel.

Threats

Threats may well include your own lack of experience in the hotel trade. This could possibly cause an initial downturn in trade while you find your feet. Other local hotels are also a threat and the introduction of a new hotel may also be problematic. You should investigate the location and what future local plans might affect you.

Details about yourselves

You should include the reasons why you are looking to buy a hotel and the history behind the decision.

If you have already visited any prospective hotels give a brief description of your visit/s. Include details of the hotel you wish to purchase and briefly explain how it matches your criteria.

Give a description of your background with full details of your previous work experience. If you plan to continue with any aspect of your present job/s give full details and explain how you will manage this alongside the management of the hotel.

Explain how your previous experience might be, or is relevant to, running a hotel. You will be surprised at what you find to include. Even staying in hotels is an experience that will help you. Just think of the times you have been unhappy with some aspect of your stay or the times when you have been delighted with the comfort of your room or the attitude of the hotel staff. It all has a bearing on how you will run your hotel.

A summary

Focus on the strengths of the business that you plan to purchase, summarising why it is such an excellent opportunity and highlighting its real potential.

An appendix

This should include any information referred to in the main body of the business plan that requires further explanation, or which is best demonstrated as a graph, spreadsheet or diagram.

Our plan included the following:

- internal floor plan, with room sizes for the hotel and for the adjoining owners' accommodation;
- the purchase price with a breakdown of the costs involved and the deposit required;
- the profit and loss account and occupancy rates;
- our personal CVs;
- internal and external photographs of the hotel.

Working out what you can afford!

This isn't as clear-cut as it sounds. It is straightforward enough to work this out on paper, but coming up with a figure and then matching it to the hotel of your dreams may prove to be a different story altogether.

Selling your own house and/or business

If your move depends upon the sale of your existing house or business, this also has a significant bearing on the outcome. You will know how much you want or need to make from the sale but is this realistic? Throw into the mix your emotions and you will begin to understand how difficult your position is.

Calculating your costs

To make matters even more troublesome you will need to work out what your costs will be. This is everything from stamp duty to solicitors to removal men.

These figures are subject to change of course, and as such you must build in a contingency.

Including your savings

You may also find that you come to a point when you realise that you will have to sink all of your savings into the new purchase. You may also discover that this isn't quite enough.

Reaching a final figure

If you have found what you consider to be the 'perfect' business you will find a way to finance it no matter what the cost. This is where the time spent on researching and investigating your target and the effort you put into your business plan will pay dividends. If you have found the right property in the right location, these will reinforce the conclusions you have drawn and will help to justify your decision.

Once you have made an offer and it is accepted, you will at least have a figure to work with. Before you have done this it is almost impossible to work out, or even find out, how much you can afford. We borrowed nearly £1m but had been looking at properties on the market for between £850k and £950k, without really knowing for sure what we could afford, not having sold our own property.

What costs to expect when making the purchase

You need to compile a list of the costs you expect to incur. A spreadsheet with your initial forecast can then be added to as you move forward with your plans. You will also find that you may have to increase or even reduce certain items. A spreadsheet will enable you to keep track of your financial position and will give you an immediate picture of your progress.

We made a forecast for each item of expenditure. In some cases we had to make an educated guess at what the cost would be. We then kept a separate line in our spreadsheet detailing the actual costs. This enabled us to compare this with our forecast.

We included the agreed purchase price for the hotel and deducted from this the finance we had raised ourselves. This gave us a final figure that we needed to raise to make the purchase.

The costs we incurred and which you can also expect are as follows.

Stamp duty

We paid 4% of the purchase price of the hotel and of the separate accommodation which became our home. There is no VAT payable on stamp duty. We are still not really sure why stamp duty has to be paid other than it is a legal requirement!

Solicitors' fees

We had a different solicitor for the commercial purchase to that for our private house sale. If the purchase of the hotel is linked to the sale of your residential property you need to factor in a cost for both solicitors. We paid £3,500 plus £500 in disbursements to the commercial solicitor and a further £900 to the solicitor for the sale of our private dwelling. Both of these figures included VAT at 17.5%.

Finding the right commercial solicitor will make life much simpler and you should be able to rely on them to do their best when representing you. Our solicitor made life reasonably easy for us, and the purchase was relatively trouble-free. You will also notice that commercial solicitors are efficient and proactive when it comes to managing your account.

Valuation/survey fees

A valuation will be required and your lender may well specify who will undertake this. The valuation looks at every aspect of the property as well as valuing the business. This in turn gives the lender an assurance they that are making the right decision in making the loan. It may also highlight any problem areas with the hotel. We paid £1,762.50 including VAT for a valuation on a property we paid £1,160,000 for.

Mortgage arrangement fees

We paid a 1% arrangement fee to our mortgage broker and an additional 1% to our lender. Most lenders will add the fee back to the overall loan. However, you should check at an early stage if they operate in this way. Our lender insisted we pay this in advance.

The broker's fee was worth every penny as without their involvement we would not be where we are today. On the other hand, paying an arrangement fee to the lender in advance puts additional strain on your budget and is payable at a time when every penny counts.

Fixtures and fittings

We paid a separate fee for fixtures and fittings. In hindsight we should not have done so. If you are asked to do the same it is advisable to ask for a full list of what is and isn't included before making any agreement.

Estate agent's fees

If you are selling your own property and this is part of the overall deal, you will need to account for the fees you have to pay to your estate agent.

Other fees

These include pre-contract searches, Land Registry fees and sundry other searches. We paid a total of £1,376, including £700 to the Land Registry.

Other costs

Hotel stock and pre-payments

You should request that the sellers furnish you with a list of the stock, which on the day you take over you expect to be the items that they leave behind to assist you in running the business. On the day you arrive they must furnish you with an up-to-date list and you should check this before you make a payment to them.

Payment should be made within an agreed period, usually three days. This should give you sufficient time to check that all the items are as they should be. Do set aside time to check the list when you arrive as it can take several days.

The sellers may also ask you to pay an amount for the payments that they have already made for advertising or for any expenditure that you will benefit from once you start to run the business. They should supply you with a list, which must include the relevant dates covered. You should also receive copies of any invoices that this refers to. You must agree this list with them ahead of your move.

We paid just under £1,500 for stock. Pre-payments amounted to £900 for items such as:

◆ advertising;

◆ overlapping costs of premises licence and for a Visit Britain rating; and

◆ telephone switchboard maintenance.

Insurance

Buildings and contents insurance will be required on exchange of contracts. This could also mean that you will have to pay a substantial premium ahead of your move. We arranged insurance through a broker and agreed to pay with post-dated cheques over a three-month period. We made the first payment ten days before we moved and the balance over a period of three months starting exactly a month after we had moved in.

It is advisable to shop around for insurance as premiums vary drastically. We had quotes from several sources, all high street names operating in the commercial market. At the lower end of the scale we were quoted £2,200 rising to £3,600 at the other.

New hoteliers are hampered by their inexperience. However, you should search exhaustively until you are satisfied that you have found the best possible deal. The internet is an excellent tool for locating commercial insurers, though word of mouth/recommendation is a preferable option.

A reputable insurer will advise you on the cover that you require which will include the basic legal requirements for insuring a hotel. Be prepared to ask and be asked lots of questions. One question that particularly baffled me concerned whether the hotel had a burglar alarm! I imagined how this would work – would you ask the last guests checking in to ensure they had set this, or would you wait till 4 a.m. for them to arrive just to be sure it was set? On a more serious note the insurance must include Public Liability and Employers' Liability cover.

A word of warning on insurance

In our first year we were offered cover for a premium of just over £2,200. At the time we felt that this was probably going to be the best price we could achieve. Having spoken to several insurers this quote came in as the lowest and the cover was as comprehensive as any other quote. You will find that commercial insurance is much more inclusive than your average household cover. You will also find that at the time you are trying to arrange this you will be very busy and it will be tempting to agree to the first quote you receive if it appears to be competitive.

We arranged cover through a broker and it was explained to us that the insurer was an American company trying to establish themselves in the UK market. This was the reason given for the premium being less than that of their competitors. We accepted this and the broker offered a variety of payment options.

A year later, half a dozen insurance brokers, all looking to win our business, approached us ahead of the renewal date. Around the same time our insurance broker contacted us and offered a premium at £100 less than the previous year. This rung alarm bells and made me suspicious. I had never heard of this type of cover going down in price. It transpired that they had charged us around £500 too much in year 1. This gave them the option to reduce the premium in year 2 and make themselves popular in the process.

One of the other brokers offered a premium of around £1,700. Included in this were items that we had previously been charged an additional premium for. They also waived their arrangement fee and offered a payment plan with monthly instalments at an exceptionally low interest rate. The offer was from the same insurance company for exactly the same policy as we had in year 1. They also agreed not to increase the premium the following year.

This deal would more than likely have been available to us if we had spent a little more time shopping around in year 1. It demonstrates that even when it appears that you have found a bargain it pays to go that one step further.

Sundry costs

Licences

We paid £110 + VAT for a food hygiene course and £152 + VAT for the personal licence course. We also paid £83 to the local council for our premises and personal licences.

Removal

You will also need to factor in the cost of moving. We paid £846 to our removal firm two weeks in advance of our move. If you are moving a long distance this will have an impact on the cost and it is often advisable to look for a local firm from the area you are moving to. They will be familiar with the area and will not have a long drive home once they have moved you in. This is beneficial if you experience problems on the day of the move and your departure is delayed.

Living expenses

We factored in the cost of our personal living expenses for the first three months.

Running costs – your first month in a new business

If you are to enjoy your first month in a new business and a new home, planning ahead is essential. The seller's expenditure is a good place to start. They will have incorporated sound financial practices ensuring that every cost of running the hotel was kept to a minimum. There is a difference between cutting corners to save money and buying from the most competitive suppliers who also offer quality assurance.

Using the previous accounting records for the hotel, you need to prepare a forecast for the expenditure for the first month. Only once you have experienced managing the hotel will you be in a position to look at reducing your overheads.

Choosing a bank for your new business

You should shop around and compare what each of the banks has to offer. Most importantly you need to find out what experience the bank you choose has with similar types of business. They all purport to be business banks but you need people who really understand you as a hotel and as a local business, and they must be accessible to discuss your needs.

Minimum requirements

If you are happy with your own bank and have a personal account, you will still need a business account and many banks offer free banking for the first year. This is the minimum requirement you should insist upon when choosing a bank. A year free sounds great on paper but a year goes by really quickly and you must ensure that you know exactly what their charges will be once the year is up.

Not only will you require a business account, you also need to arrange for card processing facilities, i.e. taking debit and credit card payments from your customers. The majority will want to pay by this method and you must be aware of the charges made for this facility. These can have a significant impact on your profit margin.

Knowing what charges will eventually be made by your bank should be a major part of your decision on who to bank with. Charges vary so much, and again, once they start to charge you for every cheque, withdrawal, direct debit and so on it soon mounts up and has a negative affect on your account balance.

We have a business manager who responds to our enquiries within a day of calling him. This is important and again should be a minimum requirement. Having to speak to a call-centre operative in a country on a different continent is not desirable. They will not know your local area or how you operate within it. Of course, having a local manager doesn't always guarantee you will receive a satisfactory response when you do speak to him or her, but at least they know who you are.

Arranging an overdraft

An overdraft can be expensive to run and isn't always the most suitable option. You need a bank that understands the hotel business and the challenges that you will face everyday. Cash flow is vital and is not that easy to control. This is why it is important to have an account that is accessible at any time of the day or night. We look at our account online everyday. This gives you an instant picture, allows you to plan for expenditure and ensures that payments are reaching your account on time.

It is nearly impossible to run a new business without some outside help, and an agreed overdraft is manageable. One of the key considerations in running your cash flow is timing, not just when direct debits or cheques leave your account but when your customers pay you.

For a week in which your guests book in on a Monday and leave on the Friday morning, all paying on that Friday by credit or debit card, it will be up to two weeks from check-in before the money hits your account. If this coincides with when payments to suppliers or to your mortgage lender are due, you need to plan ahead to ensure that you have sufficient funds in your account to cover the payments. This is where an overdraft is essential.

Keeping your own accounts

Most banks offer accounting software as part of your package and may also offer you training in how to use it. We didn't have time to look into this and having already had experience of keeping accounts didn't feel it was necessary. We do have an accountant and he prepares our tax return once a year.

However, keeping your own accounting records is relatively straightforward. We keep ours up to date and account for every month as soon after the month end as possible. Paying someone else to do this for you is a luxury, unless you really can afford to or don't have the inclination to prepare your own accounts.

Our lender has been satisfied to date with the accounting records we have prepared ourselves. We run all of our finances through our business account so our bank has an exact picture of our financial position at any given time. Significantly, so do we. We recently asked our bank to extend our overdraft just for a week to help with cash flow and they asked me to supply details of our income and expenditure! I pointed out that all they needed to do was to access my account details!

4
Considering making a purchase

What to look for when you first visit

Visiting a prospective new business venture for the first time is exciting. If, like us, you have no experience of running a hotel, a viewing is exhilarating. Once you have studied the agent's sales information on the property and made an appointment on the strength of it, you should make notes on any description, which, for any reason, draws your attention or is not clear.

Study the details of the hotel on the sales agent's website and compare this to the hotel's own website. Make notes of any differences or of anything that is apparent from the websites that is not included in the sales information. If something is missing from the sales information make a note to ask specific questions on this when you visit or when you next speak to the agent. This may give you important information and may indicate when something isn't all that it appears to be.

Details on the financial performance of the hotel should be made available to you ahead of your visit. If this information is not included in the details you have been sent, then ask for it. If this is refused, you need to find out why. There is little point in a visit if the financial situation is so dire that you wouldn't be able to make ends meet if you made the purchase. This information is often linked to the reason why the hotel is for sale.

A fact-finding mission

The first hotel we visited did not supply details on the hotel's turnover. We had made the appointment on the basis that viewing a property would be helpful and we treated it very much as a fact-finding mission. We found that the owners, a husband and wife team, had planned to run the hotel together. They had soon discovered that the husband would need to find other work if they were to continue with the project. The hotel had just five rooms and was much more a bed and breakfast than a hotel.

The owners stated that they had decided to sell because the husband did not enjoy running the hotel. On being furnished with their accounts the real reason became clear. The location of the hotel had led us to believe that occupancy levels would be high, and indeed they were adequate. However, because of the location, they had lots of competition and the business was seasonal with excellent turnover during the summer months but very little trade over the winter. Their turnover mirrored the number of letting rooms and the seasonality of the business. This did not produce sufficient turnover or have the capability of doing so to make it an attractive proposition to us.

The visit did give us the opportunity to ask questions and to find out how the business operated. It also prepared us for our next visit to a similar hotel and allowed us to ask more searching questions.

When you make your first visit try to take in as much as you can about everything you see, not just inside the building, but on the outside, the grounds, the surroundings, the location and the property's overall appearance. Try to imagine that you are a guest just arriving. Every last detail is important and you must consider everything if you are to make an informed decision.

On arrival

If you arrive by car make a note of or ask yourself these questions:

◆ How easy it is to park?

◆ Does the hotel have a car park?

◆ Did you have to park on the street?

◆ How easy or difficult was this?

◆ Are there any parking restrictions?

◆ How many cars will fit into the hotel car park?

If you arrive by taxi note the following:

◆ How far is the hotel from the train or bus station?

◆ How easy was it to find a taxi?

◆ How long did it take to reach your destination?

All of this will tell you how accessible the hotel is for its customers.

The exterior of the building

The exterior of the building will tell you whether the owners have looked after the property. Look not just at the building itself but also at the grounds and garden, the plants, the driveway and any signs. The look of the hotel is vital. Guests form an impression as soon as they arrive and the more welcoming the vista the more likely it is they will immediately feel comfortable and at ease.

The look of the property is easily forgotten in the excitement of your first visit. A photograph or video recording will enable you to look back at your visit when you are in the comfort of your own living room. It will also help you to identify any possible areas for improvement. However, do remember to ask the owners' permission to take pictures or film inside the property.

The reception area

When you enter the building make a note of how easily you gained access, whether the door was already open or if you are greeted by an intercom voice. The reception area is also key. On arrival guests spend a few minutes checking in, receiving instructions and passing the time of day with the owner. Take a good long look at how welcoming the reception area is, how it is laid out, whether the flooring is dirty or worn, if there are flowers or if there is too much clutter. Notice the smell – is it musty or fragrant or can you still smell the remnants of breakfast? Does the family dog greet you or is it barking in the background? Does the reception smell of the dog? This again will give you a feeling of what the guests experience when they arrive. First impressions are very important.

Your first visit will be fairly brief. You will know almost immediately whether the place feels right for you. You will be shown all of the bedrooms, the lounge, bar area, public toilets, dining room, kitchen and any utility rooms. You will also view your living accommodation.

Your living accommodation

Consider how your living accommodation interacts with the hotel.

♦ How easy is it to access the reception area from the owners' living space?

♦ Are the guests likely to wander inadvertently into the owners' space or is this clearly signed?

If the owners live in a separate house in close proximity to the hotel find out how the hotel guests communicate with the hotel when the owners are not on the premises. How easy is it for the owners to keep in touch with what is happening when they are not there?

> Our hotel has CCTV in the main reception and the telephone and front door intercom system can be transferred to our house or to our mobile.

If you live in

You will also need to spend time discussing what you think life will be like when you are living in the hotel. You will always be on duty and at the beck and call of your guests. You will need to be contactable at all times of the day and night. Living in the hotel has its advantages. If your guests are late arriving or they require something from you, it will not take long for you to respond to them.

Equally you will be able to keep your eye on them. Guests can and will misbehave from time to time. You will be able to answer the front door quickly and to respond to any visitors promptly. You will always know what is happening and be in a position to react to any situation.

Living in the hotel does of course have its disadvantages. If guests know that you are not far away they are more likely to call upon you for the slightest reason. This can be very frustrating. You are sharing your home with strangers and will have to put up with the different sounds and smells this involves. While guests coming home late from a night out can be disturbing, at least you will be on hand if they pose a problem.

If you live separately

Living in an adjoining property also has its pros and cons. On the positive side you have your own space to retreat into where guests cannot annoy you. You can suffer from sick building syndrome when you are always working in the same place, so a separate home is an excellent place to retire to at the end of a long day. On the negative side it is a more expensive way of living as you have the costs of running a home as well as a business. If you live in the hotel in a separate part of the building you will share many of the running costs such as lighting and heating, rates and water and repairs and renewals.

In your own home, away from the hotel you are not always in a position to know what is going on in the hotel. When we first arrived we found this extremely difficult, as we had to trust that our guests would behave late at night. We did have one particular incident a few weeks after we had taken over which made us uneasy for many weeks. Four middle-aged businessmen, who appeared to be respectable, decided to hold a party in our bar area after they had arrived home in the early hours of the morning, having attended a local function.

When they checked in they explained they were going out to dinner and asked which of the public houses catered for evening meals. They also enquired about our bar closing time and said they would be back before 11 p.m. and might require a nightcap. They were in fact attending a black tie function which ended at midnight.

On arriving at 6.30 the next morning to prepare for breakfast, we found the bar area in chaos. As the bar area doubles as reception we were concerned that other guests would see the turmoil when they came down for breakfast. The bar was covered in empty water and beer bottles, two of our chairs were broken and one was covered in vomit. The umbrella stand was full of water and what appeared to be blood, and the front door and adjacent wall were also stained with blood. The floor was awash.

On closer inspection of the immediate vicinity we discovered five men asleep in the guests' lounge, two of whom were not our guests. Three were fully stretched out on the sofas still suited and with their shoes on. The other two were asleep upright in armchairs. There were empty beer bottles and glasses all over the room.

So what would you do in this situation? Living next door we did not hear the guests come in or make any noise. We had no forewarning that they would behave in this way. Our immediate reaction was to clear up the bar area to ensure other guests did not witness the carnage. At the same time we had to start to prepare for breakfast.

If we had lived on the premises we would have heard the commotion and been in a position to do something about it. This would have reduced the effect they had on our other guests. On the other hand, we might have inflamed the situation. People in a drunken state do not take kindly to being asked to keep the noise down and to go to bed. They are very difficult to manage even when normally they are reasonable people.

We did not hear anything and slept soundly. We could have received a call from an angry guest complaining about the noise. In this instance the guest who was kept awake and who was concerned about what was going on decided not to contact us. She did, however, seriously consider calling the police as at one stage it sounded to her as if the guests were having a disagreement and a fight. Indeed they actually were. The guest decided to do nothing, as she was concerned for us and didn't want us to be disturbed. In hindsight we were pleased with her decision, as it was much easier to sort out the mess first thing in the morning when everyone was sober and suffering from a hangover.

These types of incident are thankfully few and far between. It is how you deal with the problem that counts.

We cleared up the mess and then turned on the main light in the lounge to wake the sleepers. Not one of them stirred. Turning on the TV also had no effect. It was annoying that those asleep on the sofas still had their shoes on which were making a mess of the upholstery, though it was more annoying that they were not actually guests. They had to be shaken from their sleep and asked politely to leave. This also had no effect whatsoever. It was clear that they were all hungover and not in the mood to be disturbed.

The female guest arrived on the scene and explained what she had heard. She was a regular customer so we waived her bill for the night as an apology. Thankfully she was very understanding and she continues to stay with us.

With no sign of movement in the lounge it was time for more direct action. None of the sleepers appeared to pose a physical threat and as such it was relatively safe to become agitated with them. Within a few moments the gatecrashers had been ejected and the guests banished to their rooms to pack. We refused to serve them breakfast.

On checking out, the managing director of the troublemakers began an argument over how much damage they had actually caused. By clearing up after them it was not obvious to him that anything had actually occurred. Eventually, following a heated discussion in which we pointed out that we were a respectable, professional, family-run hotel and did not welcome such appalling behaviour from grown men that should know better, as well as the fact that we had CCTV footage of events, he finally relented and paid the bill plus £250 compensation.

We wrote immediately to the person responsible for making the booking and issued a lifetime ban for the entire company. They have not been back. More importantly we learned a valuable lesson in how to manage difficult situations. We analysed every stage of how we reacted to the problem and this still helps us to manage guests more effectively. Sometimes it is just not possible to know in advance how guests will behave. It is important to learn from every new experience.

It is unlikely that the owners of the hotel you are visiting will relate any experiences like this one to you. However, you should be aware that from time to time you will have to deal with awkward customers. It doesn't hurt to ask the owners about the type of guests they usually attract. Are they mostly young, middle-aged, male or female? Do they work for local businesses or visit to attend events? This type of information will enable you to build a picture of the daily life in the hotel.

The rooms

All of the rooms in the hotel are important and will indicate to you how well run the hotel is and how comfortable it is for guests. On your visit, note the decor in each room and how well maintained this is. Inspect as closely as is polite how clean and tidy the en-suite bathroom is and what toiletries are included as standard. Check out the linen, the carpets and curtains and the furniture in each bedroom. Try to see whether these are new or old and in good repair. Some of these items may need to be replaced straightaway if they are not up to your standards.

Look at the courtesy tray in the bedrooms and note what is included and if these are clean. Check out the condition of the kettle and its cord and look to see if the cup and saucer or mug is clean and not chipped. Again you may have the expense of changing these.

If the bedrooms and hallways are carpeted you need to look to see if there are any seriously worn patches or if they are particularly dirty or stained. Hiring a specialist to clean the carpets or buying new can be expensive and you may have to factor this into your start-up costs.

If you get the chance, inspect the window frames and note if these need replacing or repainting. Look under a bed and behind a wardrobe to see if these have been dusted. This will tell you how well cared for the hotel has been.

The common areas

The common areas used by guests should be clean at all times. They are in constant use and as such the guests will notice if a tea stain hasn't been cleared up or an empty beer bottle is left at the side of the sofa or armchair. If there is a guests' lounge make a note of how many guests may use the room at any given time and make a mental list of the facilities such as the TV, DVD or music system.

Your visit will, no doubt, be arranged for late morning, lunchtime or early afternoon as this is likely to be the most convenient time for the owners. They will have cleared breakfast and made a start or finished making up the bedrooms by then. There should be no excuse for any untidiness and the hotel will be in a state of readiness. This is how guests will find the hotel when they arrive to check in.

The dining room and/or breakfast area

The dining room is a key area as guests spend the most important part of the day here. With the owner showing you the hotel it will be difficult to look under the tables and check whether the chairs are free from breadcrumbs. If you find the right moment ask if you could have a wander round on your own.

As the dining room is so important try to spend as much time here as you can. Make a note of the table layout, the linen, the cutlery and crockery, and the level of cleanliness. Ask at what time of day breakfast is served and what is provided. If there is a menu on view ask if you may take a copy.

Remember that each guest spends the first 15 to 30 minutes of their day in this room; at weekends they will spend longer. Look at the view from each table. Is this a view that would please you first thing in the morning? Tables with a view of the outside world will be more popular than those with an inward view. You may need to change the layout to give more of your guests this outlook.

The kitchen area

The kitchen should also be clutter-free and clean. Whether the hotel offers just breakfast or half or full board you need to consider the size of the kitchen, the layout and the appliances available. The more meals a day offered to guests the more wear and tear on the kitchen and the appliances.

The kitchen should be clean within an hour of breakfast or dinner finishing. There is no excuse for leaving dirty crockery and cutlery or pots and pans for any length of time. Equally all surfaces should be spotless and any appliances should be cleaned regularly.

If the kitchen is dirty at a time of day when you would expect it to be clean you need to try to find out why. If the proprietor has a cook or chef and waiting staff, it might be that they have not been supervised or trained effectively. If he or she is running the kitchen and doing all of the cooking and cleaning they might be understaffed and not have the time to clean the kitchen properly. If this is the case ask them for details of their staff and their schedule for preparing meals. Again this is something you may want or have to change.

Public areas

If the hotel has public areas such as a bar or lounge find out if these are open to the public or are exclusive to guests. Note the format of each area, what furniture is included and what facilities are available to guests. And look at the level of cleanliness and the state of repair.

Keeping up standards

We have two public toilets, which are available to guests when they are in our bar or lounge and do not want to go back to their room. We keep these clean at all times and refresh the toiletries and towels every day. Any area used by your guests outside their bedrooms must be kept in this way, as this will make a lasting impression.

On your first visit you will probably not be given much time to dwell in any one place for very long. If two of you are visiting you should agree before the visit what each of you will look at and what questions to ask. Preparing in this way will help you to cover as much ground as possible. If you like what you see first time round you will no doubt be back a second time. On a second visit you can expect to have a much closer look.

Going back for more

We visited our hotel on several occasions over the course of a four-month period, though we made an offer after the second visit. On our third visit we took our two children with us. Our five-year-old had concerns with the first two properties we viewed and we wanted to ensure that he would be happy. On our fourth visit we met with our potential lender. On our fifth we took our parents. On our sixth we took another potential lender. We visited alone on the seventh visit just to make 100% sure of our decision and to spend the day looking at the town and other local villages. The eighth and final viewing entailed spending the day with the proprietor running through management issues and asking hundreds of questions.

On every visit we viewed the entire premises. We also noted that the proprietor took several telephone calls during each of our visits. Many of these involved customers making a booking and we considered this to be a sign that business was brisk. We do receive calls throughout the day and no one time is busier than another. When you are visiting, note how many times the telephone rings and how each call is answered. Whenever people call they expect a hotel to present a professional, helpful and friendly manner.

What questions to ask the seller

Before you make an offer your questions should cover such things as turnover and occupancy and how many staff they employ. You must ask to see the trading figures for the past three years and discuss progress. You should ask about the type of guests that stay, where they come from, whether they are tourists or businessmen or a mix of both, how many nights on average each guest stays at the hotel and if there are any customers or companies that place regular business.

Initially you must ask questions that are designed to give you a detailed picture of the success of the business. Once you have made an offer and this has been accepted, the questions will be of a more practical nature and will involve the day-to-day management of the hotel.

It is entirely up to you how you interpret each of the answers that you receive. If the owner has nothing to hide they will answer you truthfully and in full. There will always be something they don't want you to notice or find out about. This might be vital; equally, it could be trivial. The questions you pose must be searching and far reaching to ensure you discover as much as there is to know.

Occupancy

Occupancy alone will tell you if the hotel is successful and popular. You should be given details of the occupancy for three years or for however long the hotel or proprietor has been trading. These will give you an idea of when the hotel is at its busiest and at its quietest.

You should ask for clarification on this, as you need to discover why the hotel is busy at certain times and not at others. If you do so you will then be able to make plans on how to improve occupancy. It may simply be that at particular times of the week, month or year you will never be able to attract custom. If so, you will know when you can take a rest, a holiday or undertake repairs or decorating.

If occupancy levels are falling you need to ask the owner why they think that this is happening. There may be a host of different reasons. They may not want to tell you. You need to be convinced that it is not a decline that is set to continue. After all, you do not want to take over a failing business that even the most renowned hotelier in the world could not reverse. It is more than likely that there is a reason and that you will be able to address this successfully with a simple adjustment.

The fabric of the building

You should also ask about the fabric of the building. A survey and valuation will show up any major problems. There is no harm in asking when the roof was last replaced, what insulation is in the loft, how old the kitchen appliances are and if they are covered by a guarantee.

Staff

Also ask about the staff – how long they have been employed and whether they are local. Local staff are more likely to arrive on time and be willing to work extra shifts. They will also know of friends and family looking for work and will know the area and what it has to offer.

Employing staff

Up until recently we had only ever taken on people that have been recommended to us by our existing staff. If we need someone new we always approach the staff in the first instance. This saves time and money and you are not likely to be disappointed with the person you take on. They are less likely to let you down if the person who recommended them also works for you.

When you visit again after your offer has been accepted it might be possible to meet any existing staff. On the other hand, the sellers may wish to keep the sale private and not inform staff until much nearer the time of your ownership. This is normal procedure as anything could happen and they may not wish to unsettle the people working for them. We met the housekeeper and cleaner on our final visit.

It is unlikely that you will learn very much from meeting the staff in advance as they will be guarded in any conversations, especially if the proprietor is with you at the time and they will not want to upset the applecart. We used the opportunity to reassure the staff. We let them know that they would be needed and that we had no intention of changing the way in which they worked. Even if you plan to change everything this will put them at their ease. You have no way of telling what the sellers have told them about you or your plans. Equally, the owners are not likely to tell you if they have a problem with a particular member of their staff.

Our new cleaner was 74 years of age and rather concerned that we would not want to have somebody of this age working for us. On the contrary, she is invaluable. Having been a landlady of her own hotel for 14 years, her experience was much needed. You should also note that on takeover, legally you are not allowed to terminate any of the existing personnel's contracts.

Marketing

Ask how the hotel is being marketed, what advertising has already been agreed and if this is paying dividends. If the owners have agreed on advertising in advance you will have to pay for the period covered once you have taken over. For a small hotel it is unlikely that the owners will have embarked on a lengthy and expensive campaign.

It is important to discover which method of marketing has been the most successful as you may well decide to continue with it. Certainly in the first few weeks and months you will want to do so until you have discovered for yourselves which path to take.

What we asked on our final visit

Detailed below are the questions we asked on our final visit, just a couple of weeks before we took over. The answers gave us a more accurate picture of what was in store for us. They also highlighted areas we needed to address immediately.

It is vital that you arrange to meet with the owners in advance of your ownership and ask them as many questions as you can. *If we had not done so our start to the hotel industry would almost certainly have been a disaster and one that would have taken us weeks, if not months, to recover from.*

The questions covered the main entrance to the hotel, the guests, the staff, the hotel and its grounds, the cellar, the private living accommodation and other general issues. All of the answers we received helped us to run the hotel from the moment we took over and continued to assist us daily over the course of the first weeks of ownership.

Main entrance to hotel

- ◆ How does the front door lock?
- ◆ Are guests issued with a key to the front door?
- ◆ At what time is this locked at night?
- ◆ How does the cash till work?
- ◆ How many bar sales do you do?

- What beers/wines do you sell the most of?
- What stock will be included on takeover?

The guests

- What is the telephone number for the card payment terminal?
- What is the telephone number for the private accommodation?
- What percentage of debit/credit card/cheque payments do you take?
- Do you offer a cash back facility?
- When does the contract for your card system end?
- What forward bookings are there?
- How are guests registered at check-in, i.e. what forms are used, etc.
- What booking forms are available when guests arrive?
- Are guests asked to pay a deposit?
- Do you process credit card payments at the end or beginning of the guests stay?
- How many of the guests pay by cheque?
- How do you process payments by cheque?
- Do you take the customer's credit/debit card number on telephone bookings?
- Do you make a surcharge for credit card payments?
- Is there a computer record of guest bookings or just a diary?
- Can you supply a list of businesses that stay regularly?
- Do any of the regular guests have any special requirements or needs?
- When are invoices prepared?

Hotel personnel – staff

- Have the staff received any training such as food hygiene or health and safety?
- Which staff are on PAYE?
- Have staff already had or booked any holiday?

- Has any cover been arranged for staff holidays?
- Do you have any cover when you go on holiday?
- Do you pay the staff weekly or monthly?
- What method of payment do you use to pay staff?
- Do the staff work at weekends if they are needed?
- Will the staff work on the weekend of our takeover?
- Who works during the evening covering the bar and reception?
- Are any of the staff trained in first aid?

The hotel

- How does the telephone system work?
- How are guests charged for telephone calls?
- Which companies supply electricity and gas?
- Who needs to inform the cable TV company of the change of ownership?
- Which suppliers are used for food, water, newspapers, etc.?
- Which company supplies bed linen?
- Are there any existing agreements with local restaurants/hotels?
- Are there any promotional leaflets or hotel brochures available?
- Are there any printed rate cards to supply to guests or for enquiries?
- Has the previous year's tariff changed or is it likely to change in the near future?
- Which company hosts the hotel website?
- Who updates/maintains the website? Is there a contract?
- Have you undertaken a health and safety risk assessment?
- What is the fire drill procedure?
- Have any of the staff received fire safety training?
- Could we have a copy of your hotel letterhead and invoice layout?
- Have you obtained a transfer of premises licence consent form?
- What is the make of safe for insurance purposes?
- When did a qualified electrician last check the electrics?

- How does the boiler operate and when was it last serviced?
- Do you employ a local maintenance/DIY man?
- What type of paint is used on internal walls?
- Is there anything specific we need to know about the bedrooms/bathrooms?
- What items of office furniture and technical equipment are you leaving behind?
- Will my desk fit into the office or are you replacing the desk you are taking with you?
- Can you run through the main hotel electrics including fuse boxes, etc.?

The hotel grounds

- Do you lock the main gates at night and if so at what time?
- Do guests use the grounds other than for parking?
- Is there an external electrical connection?

Private accommodation

We asked to take measurements in the private accommodation as follows:
- area at top of stairs;
- kitchen table;
- curtains in children's bedroom;
- curtains in main bedroom;
- gate to coach house;
- fridge and freezer spaces;
- stair gates – kitchen door/bottom of stairs.

The hotel cellar

- How does the sump pump work?
- Is the boiler on a timer and what are the on/off times for water/heating?

General questions

◆ What time do you get up in the morning?

◆ Who cooks the breakfasts at weekends when the cook is not working?

◆ Who locks up at the end of the day?

◆ On what day are the dustbins emptied?

◆ How many dustbins do you have?

◆ Is all of the linen including the towels sent to the laundry?

◆ What duties does the housekeeper perform?

◆ Where do you shop for supplies?

Additional questions before takeover

We also made a list of additional questions that arose between our final visit and the day we arrived to take over. These were all of a practical nature involving the day-to-day management of the hotel and the companies that supplied it.

Some of the questions are repeats of the first set of questions. Either we did not have time to cover everything at the final meeting or the owners needed time to prepare their answers. Additionally some of the questions raised further points that we had not previously thought of. Our final meeting lasted all day, so be prepared and make sure you allow sufficient time to discuss every issue that concerns you.

◆ How do you deal with advance bookings?

◆ Do you have any existing agreements with local restaurants/hotels?

◆ What deal do you have with BT for the telephone system?

◆ Do you offer cash back for payment by card?

◆ Do you process credit card payments at the end of a guest's stay?

◆ Do you take a deposit on bookings?

◆ Do you take a credit card number as a guarantee on telephone bookings?

◆ Do you charge extra for credit card payments?

◆ Who are the electricity and gas suppliers?

- What happens in the evening once all guests have checked in?
- What forward bookings have been taken from the day we take over?
- How are guests charged for telephone calls?
- How many guests pay by cheque?
- Is the hotel bar popular?
- Is there a computer record of all guest bookings or just the bookings diary?
- What stock will be included in the sale?
- What percentage of guests pay by debit card?
- What is the telephone number for the card payment machine?
- Please confirm the details of the premises licence.
- Could we have a list of the regular customers?
- When can we meet the hotel staff?
- Have any of the staff booked a holiday?
- Which supplier do you use for new bed linen?
- Could we have a list of other suppliers for items such as food, water, newspapers, etc.?
- Do you have the transfer of premises licence consent form?
- Could we have contacts for the website host and web design company?
- Does the cook work at the weekend if needed?
- When will the credit card processing system end?

Last-minute news

Be prepared at the final meeting to receive news that perhaps you feel you should have been given much earlier, or news that will be of concern to you. Do not be too alarmed by this. Anything can happen in the hotel trade and often does. Something new happens nearly every day. This might be something that can change the way you think or the dynamics of the business, or it can simply be something that you have to deal with immediately, a minor maintenance problem or a staff issue perhaps.

The news we received at our final meeting gives an indication of a typical problem that can happen at any time. Just a couple of weeks before we moved we were given news that filled us with dread and caused considerable concern in the lead up to our takeover. In hindsight the news we received wasn't that much of an issue and actually worked in our favour. Similar things have happened to us over the first 18 months and we realise now that they are quite normal for this industry.

We were informed that our housekeeper, who was responsible for cleaning the hotel on a daily basis, had just had a knee operation and would be out of commission for up to two months. We immediately started to think of hiring someone to stand in for the housekeeper, perhaps through an agency. The news did not end there, however. The hotel cook had just broken her arm and we were informed that she would be off work for at least six weeks. To cap it all the owners had booked six guests to arrive on our first day and had a full hotel with 20 guests on day two. Stupidly we had assumed that the owners would not take any bookings for our first weekend. This would have given us sufficient time to settle in. We at least expected that they would have informed us of bookings a great deal earlier. In reality they could not have known in advance of the bookings when the deal would go through. We should have asked for details of bookings much earlier.

You will find that once you have settled into a routine this type of issue is not so much of a concern for you. It is how you react that is important. You will have to take action, and there is no right or wrong way in which to deal with a problem other than to think it through and plan how to overcome any obstacle to the best of your ability. If you get it wrong, the important thing to do is to learn from the experience. The next time a similar issue occurs you will be in a stronger position to deal with it.

Coping in a crisis

In our case we didn't really have many options. We asked one of the waitresses if she would cover for the housekeeper. Our questions about the staff helped us to discover that one of our waitresses started at the hotel as a cleaner. She already knew the ropes and we asked her to cover for the housekeeper. We asked the cook if she would continue to work every day and supervise us in the kitchen, not taking any active role but to direct us. Our staffing problems were over for the time being. We were very much thrown in at the deep end and had to begin our hotel life from a running start.

On the day of our move our removal firm left all of our garden furniture on the hotel lawn. They had arrived several hours ahead of us and had become impatient. Our arrival was delayed by traffic until late in the afternoon. The existing owners wanted to leave as soon as we arrived. They handed us the keys and bid us farewell. It was an exceptionally hot summer day. Our first guests were due to appear at any minute.

The questions we had asked in advance of our arrival prepared us for most of what occurred on our first weekend. We knew the process for checking in guests. We knew where all the rooms were located. We knew about the local shops, restaurants and public houses. We knew at what time the boiler was set to come on to supply hot water. We had the right number of staff in place to cater for breakfast and cleaning. We just about knew where everything was located in the kitchen. We had agreed what supplies would be left for us to enable us to cater for breakfast for several days, and we had a list of suppliers to contact when we ran out.

The sellers also left written instructions covering every area of the hotel which they had devised when they first opened. Neither of them had run a hotel before and it helped them to ensure that they maintained a routine and would be in a position to hand over to new owners with the minimum of fuss when they eventually sold. The instructions included everything from the set up of breakfast in the morning through to closing up at the end of the day.

You may also find that it is possible to spend a few days with the owners ahead of your takeover. If you spend at least a day working with them and shadowing key personnel you will learn a great deal. This will prepare you even more readily and will ease the stress of not knowing what lies ahead of you.

The main answers we received at our final meeting clarified many of our concerns and ensured a relatively straightforward first few days. They still make interesting reading some 18 months later!

Vital information

One of the most vital pieces of information we gleaned from our questionnaire concerned the central heating system. The main boiler controlling the heating and hot water was located in the hotel cellar and worked on a timer system. As it was a new boiler and just a couple of years old the owners had not arranged a maintenance agreement with a gas supplier. A gas safety certificate is a legal requirement for commercial premises so we immediately looked for a company specialising in commercial properties. Having approached the existing gas supplier for the hotel we found that they only covered domestic appliances. They did send an engineer to inspect the hotel boiler. However, it was discovered that they had no record of our type of boiler and as such they were not in a position to assist us.

Fortunately, they were able to recommend a company whom we contacted, and following two visits by their engineers we agreed a contract for 24/7 coverage of the boiler and our gas cooker. Not only is this a legal requirement but it gives piece of mind. If your heating or hot water is out of action for any time longer than a day you have a really serious problem.

Early to rise . . .

One of the more depressing answers we received concerned the owners' start time in the morning. Up until the moment we asked this question we hadn't really considered this very much. We had always said to friends and family that we had a cook who looked after breakfast, but the cook had a broken arm . . . Indeed, 5.55 a.m. is still a time we rise each weekday morning. In fact we set the alarm for 5.54 a.m. just to be different but it is still very early and not something either of us was used to. It took over a year before we really became accustomed to getting up so early.

The first winter was the most difficult. We arrived on the last day of June so it was light in the morning and didn't get dark until 10 p.m. Waking up at 5.54 on a dark and cold day in December is quite a shock. It takes real stamina to work through a long winter.

Now into our second winter we are resigned to dark mornings and dark early evenings – it now feels normal and is not nearly so depressing. It just takes a bit of time to accept your new way of life, especially if this is not part of your daily routine before you become a hotelier.

What to consider before making an offer

If you are planning to buy a hotel for the very first time and have no experience in the hotel or leisure industry you must consider how your life will change before you commit to making an offer.

Based on what you have discovered about the hotel, its financial record, its occupancy, its location and the type of business it is, you must decide if this matches or is as close a fit as possible to what you had set out to achieve. If you are making compromises, try to think about how these will affect you in the future and the impact it will have on you and the business.

You must also decide if you really do want to own and run a small hotel. You should ask each other this question time and time again until you have exhausted every angle and explored every possibility.

Making comparisons

Have you looked at similar properties and compared the purchase price with the hotel you are about to make an offer on? It is relatively straightforward to find out. Trawling the internet for commercial agencies will allow you to access this information from their websites. There are hundreds if not thousands of hotels for sale across the UK and you will be able to find several similar properties in close proximity to the hotel you plan to buy.

Timing issues

Timing is also important. You need to consider when you will be moving in to take over the business. The time of year may dictate how busy you will be when you arrive. If you arrive at the height of the season will you be able to cope? If you arrive during a quiet period will you have sufficient income to see you through to busier times?

It will take several months between making your offer and completion. You need to plan how this will affect your existing set-up. You need to ensure that you have sufficient funds available to live, as well as to guarantee that you can settle any legal fees or other bills connected to the purchase. You will also need funds available to pay for stock, pre-paid marketing and running costs for the first couple of months. This includes the mortgage!

Yet more questions

Ask yourselves the following questions before and after making an offer and discuss each one at length:

- Is the location of the hotel ideal for your customers and for you and your family?
- Does the location dictate the type of guest the hotel attracts?
- Is the hotel busy all year round?
- Is the hotel busy at certain times of the year, month, week?
- Are occupancy levels acceptable?
- How will we improve occupancy?
- Why have the owners decided to sell?
- Is this the real reason?
- Is the building in a good state of repair?
- Will we have to allocate budget to repairs and renewals?
- Are repairs required before we move in?
- Do we have any relevant experience that will help us to run a hotel?
- Is the purchase price competitive?
- What offer should we make?
- How much should we increase our offer when our initial bid is rejected?
- When do we plan to move in and take over the business?
- Do we really want to own and run a hotel?

Giving yourselves a reality check

Having doubts about your decision is only natural. Making a life change at any stage will always raise concerns and buying your own hotel is a huge step. Even if you are absolutely certain that running a hotel is something you have always wanted to do, somewhere along the line you will almost certainly find yourself questioning your sanity. What's more, you will find that even if you don't do this, your nearest and dearest will.

Asking yourself if buying and running a hotel is definitely for you will not necessarily give you a true answer. It is only natural to have doubts. If you have never run a hotel or not even worked for yourselves before, the prospect of being in an unknown environment will be daunting.

We certainly didn't know what we were letting ourselves in for, even though we continually questioned our decision and had conducted extensive research.

If possible, speak to people who have already been through the experience and ask for their honest opinion. Ask them whether they regret the decision and more importantly why. If time permits ask them to describe a normal day from when they wake up to when they go to bed. Try to get a feel for what will be expected of you.

The fundamental questions to answer

Apart from the obvious, 'do we really want to do this?' question, you should ask yourselves whether you are willing to be out of bed by 6 a.m. every day of the week and whether you are prepared always to be tied to the business. These are two key issues. If you are not happy with either answer then you must question whether you are suited to running a hotel.

You are always on call 24 hours a day, seven days a week. Even when you have no guests you must be prepared to answer the front door or the telephone and to monitor your e-mails. If enquiries do not receive a reasonably quick response this will leave the wrong type of impression.

If you have an evening receptionist or someone to stand in for you when you take a break, you will still be subject to the occasional interruption. You may also receive late evening calls or even calls in the middle of the night. Thankfully this doesn't happen too often; however, you must be prepared to answer any enquiry at any time in a professional and polite manner. First impressions count regardless of when the call arrives – even if this is at 3 a.m.! We receive the occasional call at two or three in the morning, though these are usually from someone in a different time zone who hasn't considered the time of day. This is what happens when people call a hotel – they expect it to be open all of the time!

Getting up at 6 a.m. every day is not something that everyone can do. If you are running a business your guests rely on you and expect you to be where you say you will be at any given time. It takes stamina and determination to be up at 6 a.m., especially during the winter when it is cold and dark.

If you enjoy your lie-ins or find it difficult to get out of bed before 8 a.m. you must consider how you will adapt to your new life style.

Do you have the personality to run a hotel?

The most important questions will depend on your personality and what you already do for a living. One of the most important, if not *the* most important, aspects of running a hotel is the people – and not just the people that work for you but the guests who stay with you. You will be working with your staff every day of the year and they will rely on you for their living. You will meet new guests everyday and will need to be cheerful and polite and willing to meet their demands whenever you have cause to speak to them.

Consider the impact on your family

If you have a family you must consider the impact the new life will have on them. We were not prepared to bring our two young children up living in a hotel. It was essential to us that they had their own separate living space away from our customers, and not just for their sakes but also for the sake of our guests. Business people do not necessarily want to be bothered with children running around or being woken by a crying child in the middle of the night.

You should also consider your parents or siblings and other family members and how they will be affected. If you are moving a long distance it may well be of concern. It will be difficult to see them as often as you do now. Making time for family when you are running a business will create its own challenges. It will not be possible just to drop everything and rush off to a family party or to visit a sick relative when you want to or when they expect you to.

Arranging time off

Having a holiday or even time off will be nigh on impossible in the first couple of years. Leaving your hotel for even a couple of days is difficult, even if you have left someone capable in charge. Finding someone trustworthy to stand in for you takes time, unless you already have someone lined up whom you know and trust.

Summing up

All of these issues are surmountable and it is possible to enjoy your new life. It takes time to adapt. You will question, on a regular basis, why you have made such a drastic change, until you finally feel comfortable with your new lifestyle.

5
Making an offer and what happens next

Making an offer

The asking price for the business will depend on a number of key factors. Your key concern should be whether your offer is within your means and will at the same time be attractive to the sellers.

If you have already researched other similar properties and studied the hotel market generally, you will have a feel for whether your offer will be taken seriously.

You must convince yourselves that the asking price is fair and that it reflects the true value of the business. Most commercial agents will price a property competitively at a tariff that will attract serious buyers. Overpricing will deter most prospective purchasers. The price will also depend on the success of other recent sales of similar properties.

Your budget will dictate whether your target is within your price range. If you decide to attempt a purchase above your budget you must be certain that the business will be profitable enough to withstand even the smallest increase in interest rates or that your influence on the business will be sufficiently positive to improve turnover. There is absolutely no point in buying a hotel or making an offer based purely on emotions. You must weigh up all possible angles and be convinced that you are making a business decision. Unless of course money is no object!

Accounting for goodwill

You must account for goodwill. This may well be built into the asking price. If it is, you should determine whether this truly represents value to you as new owners.

When we made an offer the sellers had only been trading for just over two years and as such could not include goodwill. A hotel must be trading for at least three years for this to be included in the asking price.

Building in a buffer

You should also build into your offer a buffer. This will allow you to make an increased offer if your first is turned down and give you some starting capital for when you take over the business.

Making an offer

Our first offer was turned down. However, we were prepared for this and our second slightly increased offer was accepted. We were happy with our second offer, even though it was slightly more than we could afford. We considered that the business had potential and that we could build upon this. All of the other key factors including location and occupancy made us comfortable that we had made the right decision.

What happens once the offer is agreed?

Once your offer has been formally accepted you will need to organise your mortgage offer or arrange for the relevant finance to be in place. You will also need to instruct solicitors. If your move depends on the sale of your own property you may have an anxious wait until it is finally sold.

Buying and selling

We placed our house on the market as soon as our offer on the hotel was accepted. We did not see much point in selling our home until we were ready to finalise a deal on a hotel.

It took several months to sell our home and several changes of estate agent until we found the right one! Again, the timing of your offer will dictate the speed at which the purchase and your eventual move will take place. Our commercial agency advised us that the usual timeframe for a sale of a hotel is six to nine months from the date when the hotel is first placed on the market.

We made an offer in October 2005 and finally moved into our hotel at the end of June 2006. By keeping in contact with the owners, via their solicitors, we informed them of our progress at every stage. At one point we were concerned that our own home would not sell. It had been on the market for several weeks and we had had very few viewings. We relayed this to the sellers and assured them that we would soon be in a position to move forward.

Again, timing played a part. Selling a house over the Christmas period is not easy and it was not until the early New Year that we started to make progress. Additionally we needed to sell at a price that would enable us to meet the purchase price of the hotel.

Contacting the sellers

If you make contact with the sellers directly, first ensure that they are happy for you to do this. They may not want you to speak to their staff until after completion. If they agree to direct contact be wary of the number of times that you speak with them and the reasons for your contact. We preferred to speak directly to the owners as it gave us an instant picture of what was actually happening. We always called in the afternoon when we knew that their staff had finished work.

Following the offer

Once your offer is accepted you will have a realistic budget to work with. You will be in a position to plan and to make informed decisions on all of the related costs.

Your commercial solicitor will guide you through the course of events that follow an offer. A valuation of the hotel will take place and you will be required to meet the mortgage lender to discuss the terms of any loan. You will be required to submit your business proposal to the lender and this must include all data on the hotel including details of the purchase price and the hotel's accounts.

Once our business plan had been accepted we met with the lender at the hotel. The owner gave us a guided tour and following this we discussed the loan with the lender and our broker in the guests' lounge. Following this meeting a valuation of the property took place. The valuer was recommended by our broker and approved by the lender and this cost us £1,500 plus VAT.

If you have agreed to purchase fixtures and fittings separately you must ask the sellers for a complete list of what is included at the earliest possible time. The cost should be included in your budget as part of the purchase price.

Making an offer and having it accepted is exciting. Making the right offer for you, both in terms of the price and the type of property, will determine your future. Don't forget to celebrate!

What about the vendors?

The sellers will also be making a big decision. For whatever reason they have decided to sell, it too will have a major impact on their future.

Reasons for selling

Our sellers purchased the property as an investment and as a retirement project. The property had been residential for some 300 years and had fallen into decline in recent times. They spent nearly four years refurbishing the property, turning it into a hotel. They developed some of the land and converted two of the outbuildings to residential use. They sold one conversion and lived in the other.

They had a specific reason for selling. They had built the business successfully over a relatively short space of time. They had established the hotel as superior accommodation for the business traveller and had scores of regular customers. Their occupancy level was respectable and above the national average at the time of 63%.

If you have established why your sellers have decided to call it a day and you are happy that this is the true reason, this information can help you. You will no doubt plan to build on any previous success and improve what the hotel has to offer. The most obvious pointer to the reason for a sale is the turnover and occupancy level. Whatever the sellers tell you, these figure do not lie and they will give you a more reliable benchmark.

If the sellers have struggled to make ends meet this could be for a number of reasons. The turnover and occupancy levels will tell you if you can make the business work for you. The sellers may have borrowed too much initially and only be selling as a result of not being able to meet rising mortgage and overhead payments. They may have had unexpected costs for repairs and renewals. The turnover and occupancy will tell you if you can afford to run the business effectively. This will also indicate where you can make improvements. You might find that weekend occupancy is poor or certain months of the year are quiet.

The sellers might be moving to pastures new and to a more challenging venture. They may have decided that hotel ownership is not for them. It could be that the hotel is not attracting sufficient custom. It might be that the owners do not have what it takes to be in the hotel business. It is important for you to discover the real reason and the accounts are the best place to start.

Checking the accounts

You should ask to see as much management accounting information as they are prepared to give you. Start with the previous three years' accounts and ask for a record of occupancy figures. The sellers are required to furnish you with this information and you will not want to go ahead with a purchase or even make an offer if this information is not readily available. Equally your lender will need this information if they are going to be in a position to lend you the money.

Contacting the vendors

The sellers may not want contact with you other than through your solicitor. You should respect this at all times. It is reasonable for you to visit the hotel and inspect your purchase as many times as is acceptable to the seller. We visited our hotel on eight separate occasions and each time the seller facilitated our visit without any complaint or problems.

Gaining family approval

Part of your decision process may well involve the approval of your family. Taking your parents, children or a relative to visit the hotel is a valuable exercise and may throw up questions you have not previously considered.

Getting information

The sellers will want to reassure you that you have made a wise choice and will wish to accommodate most reasonable requests for information. They will want to work with you in ensuring that your purchase is successful and completion is achieved with the least amount of hurdles.

Do ask as many questions as you can. Arrange to meet with the sellers to discuss the day-to-day management of the hotel. They may also be willing to let you spend a day or two, or possibly longer, working alongside them. This would give you the best possible start, as it will throw up new questions and situations that had not previously occurred to you.

Keeping the business running

You can also expect the sellers to keep the business running smoothly and at least at the same level of turnover as before they accepted your offer. They will, after all, be looking to make as much money as possible before the handover. It is in their interests to keep trading to make the most of the business.

Reaching the point of no return – planning ahead

You will reach a point of no return – the point at which you are committed to making the purchase. You will have paid for a valuation, paid a deposit to your solicitor, agreed to pay an arrangement fee to your broker if you have one, and started to make payments for courses and to local authorities. If you work for someone else you will have handed in your notice. If you work for yourself you will be winding down your existing business and letting customers and suppliers know of your plans. You will have told friends and family and may even have organised a farewell party.

You will be in the middle of contacting all and sundry, arranging removals and speaking to licensing and other relevant authorities. You should now be planning what to do when you move in and start to run the business. You should ask the sellers if it would be possible to speak to your new staff. You should plan what you are going to say to them before you meet them.

Staff and wages

We met the two most senior staff members, our housekeeper and our cleaner. We reassured them both that we would continue to run the hotel as normal and that their jobs would be safe. We pointed out that we would be relying on them and that we looked forward to working with them. If you have no experience of running a hotel your key personnel are invaluable to you. You should also be aware that it is a legal requirement to retain all contracted staff.

We looked into running our own payroll and considered all of the information sent to us by the local authority to decide whether this would save us time and money. Unless you already have experience of accounting for PAYE this can be time-consuming, although filing your own PAYE online does have its rewards in the form of an allowance for doing so. We decided to employ an independent PAYE company. The allowance is still given and we pay £75 a quarter for the service. Each week we send an e-mail with details of the hours worked by each staff member and in return we receive an e-mail with payslips including the income tax and national insurance deductions. Once a quarter we receive a report of the amount due to be paid in respect of tax and NI, and we send a cheque to cover this. This saving in time is a much simpler system and to us represents good value.

Your commercial solicitor will keep you updated of any developments and you will be required to sign documentation. You should read everything they send to you and take your time with this. We read all documents at least twice and we asked questions if we were unsure of anything. It is tempting just to skim through the vast amounts of paperwork and assume that your solicitor would tell you if there was any cause for concern. While this may well be the case it is important to know as much as you can about the property you are purchasing and the financial arrangement that you will be entering.

We found that one of the documents sent to us made specific mention of Chancel Repair. In our naivety we had not heard of this before. We also noted in the environmental report that the South West had a significant problem with radon gas. Again we had no previous knowledge of this.

Chancel Repair

Chancel Repair refers to an ancient bye-law which allows the church to levy fees from its parishioners for repairs. There is no legal argument against this. If the church decides to send you an invoice for repairs to its roof you have to pay up. There have been several recent legal battles involving people who didn't want to pay and took the matter to court. Each time the church won the case. It does sound unfair but until the legal loophole is closed this is something you need to take seriously. Your solicitor will advise you that insurance cover for Chancel Repair is available. They will also advise that a search is possible to discover what percentage chance you have of being exposed to Chancel Repair.

Insurance is available only by arranging this with your solicitor. It is not possible to arrange this privately. Thankfully the insurance premium is a one-off payment covering you for the duration of your ownership. Our search report advised that the hotel was not in an area affected by Chancel Repair and our solicitor advised that insurance would not be necessary.

Radon gas

Radon gas affects only certain areas of the UK. The West and South West have many areas seriously affected. Radon is naturally occurring, and is a colourless and odourless radioactive gas found at varying levels in all houses in the UK and across Europe. An online search will give you access to all of the relevant information you need to discover if you will be affected.

Health and safety in a commercial property dictates that you must protect your staff and of course your customers from the effects of radon.

Radon comes from the minute amounts of uranium occurring naturally in all rocks and soil. It is present in all parts of the United Kingdom. Normally the gas disperses outdoors so levels are generally very low. In certain areas geological conditions can lead to higher than average levels.

It should be noted that while exposure to the gas is not normally a health risk, exposure to particularly high levels of radon might increase the risk of developing lung cancer.

If you are concerned that radon may pose a health risk to anyone connected with your hotel you should contact an agency that can test for indoor levels to confirm whether remedial action is required.

We contacted the Health Protection Agency. Their website can be found at www.hpa.org.uk.

The HPA sent us radon detectors, which are small and can be placed in the property without causing any alarm or inconvenience. The detectors are left in place for three months and then returned for analysis. The results arrive a few weeks later and you are then in a position to decide what action to take. Our results negated the need for any action.

The HPA advises that the most effective way to deal with radon is to fit a 'radon sump' to vent the gas into the atmosphere. The sump has a pipe connecting a space under a solid floor to the outside and sucks the radon from under the property expelling it harmlessly into the atmosphere.

The cost of the testing in September 2006 was £38.78 – a small price to pay for peace of mind.

It is advisable to take immediate action when you receive any form of notification or documentation from any source connected to your move. The sooner you deal with what is required of you the sooner you will be in a position to complete your purchase.

Arranging buildings and contents insurance

On completion you will need to arrange for buildings and contents insurance. This will require you to have details of the build of the property, a full list of all of the contents and any security in place such as fire/smoke alarm systems, CCTV and burglar alarms. The insurance company will also ask you about the local emergency services and the distance to the nearest fire and police stations.

Transferring utilities

The hotel accounts will give you access to data on the cost of rates and water, gas and electric, and the premises licence. You will need to contact all of the agencies concerned to let them know the date that you will be taking over. You should establish the cost for the coming year for all services provided to the hotel and make decisions on whether you decide to contract these from new sources. Be aware that initially you may be required legally to honour any existing contract for a specified period and as such you will be tied to particular companies whether you like it or not.

Arranging licences

When your moving date is confirmed you will have a short period in which to organise everything you need to ensure a smooth takeover. It is advisable to have completed any training and qualifications you need well in advance of the moving date. You will need to finalise details of the premises licence, the alcohol licence and your personal licence to sell alcohol before you move. Contact should be made with the local authorities to ascertain when they require you to supply personal data and to complete the required paperwork. This all takes time and working on this well in advance of your confirmed moving date will be much less stressful than leaving it to the last minute.

Managing the hotel before you move in!

If what you have read so far is daunting, you should take into account that you will be employing a solicitor and that you will be paying them for a service. Choosing the right commercial solicitor will ensure that you receive the best possible advice and service at all times. We still speak to our solicitor on a regular basis even though we moved 18 months ago.

You will also be dealing with a lender and they will want you to succeed. As such they will work with you to ensure that the move and the business is a success.

As well as organising all of the legal requirements, taking the various qualifications and reading up on health and safety, you also need to consider how you will operate as hoteliers from day one.

Getting to know our new surroundings

We contacted all of the services for the local area including the police, the fire brigade and the local council. We asked them to come and see us in the week we arrived at the hotel and for any information they had on what they expected from us.

We visited the town where our hotel is located and spent the day there. We visited some of the neighbouring villages, toured the business parks in the next town and had lunch in one of the nearby cafés. This helped us to acclimatise to our new environment and gave us the opportunity to see how busy the town was.

We took note of how many people were in the main high street, how many cars were parked, the parking restrictions, the shops, the distance to the railway station and the location of the nearest shopping centre. We visited our son's new school and walked the route we would soon become accustomed to. We had already met the head teacher on a previous visit and had been lucky enough to confirm a place for our son at the school nearest to the hotel.

Making plans from day one

You should also make plans for the day you arrive and for the first few weeks. This should include arranging for your staff to be available to work and for any suppliers to be advised of your requirements. If you have guests in residence from the moment you arrive, make plans for how you will cater for them. If you will be checking them in, make sure you have sufficient registration forms available.

If the hotel is full try to arrange for all of your cleaning and waitress staff to work for you for the first few days. You will be unfamiliar with your new surroundings and it will take you several days to settle in. Even if you have arranged to work in the hotel with the owners for a couple of days prior to your visit, it will still take time to know where everything is kept and how your staff work. It can take a few months before you feel totally comfortable and aware of what is required of you.

It is difficult to arrange for the hotel to be empty for the first few days. It is tempting to do this as it would give you time to settle in and to explore. In reality it is a better option to be busy as you learn more quickly and you can monitor your staff in action. It is an opportunity to get your hands dirty and show that you are willing to be involved with all aspects of the hotel, from cooking breakfast to cleaning rooms. The more you involve yourselves at an early stage the sooner you will become accustomed to your new life.

Up and running from day one!

On the day we arrived we had six guests to check in and a further 14 the following day. The hotel was full from day two. We had no other option than to get on with it. Looking back this was undoubtedly the best thing for us though it didn't feel like it at the time.

We agreed with the owners that they would arrange for sufficient supplies to be available to cover breakfast for the first five days and for laundry for the same period. Our meeting with them just two weeks before the move helped us to discover what we needed to do to ensure that the hotel was up and running from day one.

Arranging payment facilities

One of the most important items is the credit/debit card payment set up. If you need to set up a new business bank account you must do this in the lead up to the move and it must be in place before you begin to run the hotel. Many banks offer free banking for the first year or two, and some offer free banking without a time limit. A free banking period of a year ends sooner than you expect and charges can affect cash flow if not managed effectively.

Many organisations offer card-processing facilities. You should shop around for the best deal. Service providers always ask for your projected turnover and say that they base their charges on this. If you decide to offer your customers the option to pay by any of the main cards, you will find that some cards attract a higher fee than others.

> We offer guests the opportunity to pay by all of the major credit and debit cards. Our monthly commission fee for this in year two is on average £180; however, in our first year of trading the average was £220.

Special deals

Some banks offer a special deal for first-time customers and some of the leisure trade associations offer a special or discounted rate if you become a member. If this is your first time utilising such a service your negotiating power will be much less than commercial users with a track record. Whichever service you choose you must factor monthly commission payments into your budget from the outset.

Service fees

Most providers charge a monthly service fee and again this can vary from company to company. Often the fee is higher if the commission charged is low in comparison to other companies. A simple calculation will demonstrate which is your best option. Bear in mind that you can revisit the charges and renegotiate with your chosen provider after the first year, or sooner if you feel brave!

Negotiating the best deal

We began with one company and after eight months asked them if they would lower their commission charges. They refused and we had to wait until a year had passed before asking them again as our agreement included a clause which allowed us to cancel at any stage but with a financial penalty.

After a year they refused to negotiate again, informing us that our turnover was not sufficient for them to lower their charges, so we shopped around. We found a more competitive company and agreed a deal equivalent to a 20% saving. In the spirit of fairness we contacted our existing supplier – and of course changing card companies involves meetings and paperwork and getting used to using a new card machine. Our existing supplier then had a change of heart and asked us to prove to them that we had received a better offer.

In the end we decided to change supplier and although we had to pay £200 to cancel the contract we saved this amount with our new supplier in the first quarter.

Accepting cheques

You also need to decide whether you will accept cheques. Some people still use this method and if you require a deposit from a customer they will sometimes send you a cheque. It is difficult to refuse any method of payment, as you will want to make life easy for your guests, but accepting a cheque will cost you time and money.

Many retail outlets now refuse to accept cheques as most people have become used to using cards or cash. Over 95% of our revenue comes from card payments and in 18 months we have banked only a handful of cheques. Banks now charge for accepting a cheque and unless you visit the bank personally you will have to incur postage.

Allowing time to clear payments

It should be noted that your cash flow will be affected by the length of time it takes the bank to credit your account with payments received. This can vary depending on which bank you are with. It also depends on the type of card – one card in particular can take up to 12 days to reach your account.

We recently banked a payment of £726 which didn't arrive in our account till 13 days later. Admittedly the payment was received four days before Christmas but you would expect it to arrive before 3 January. You must be aware that this can occur. Most cards take three to four days. If a payment is received on a Thursday it may take until the following Wednesday to reach your account. It is essential to make allowances for this and to monitor your account online every day.

Supplying invoices

You will also need invoices to give to guests in receipt of payment. If you are already VAT registered you will be aware of the legal requirements for invoice formats. If you have a VAT registration number this will appear on your invoices and so you will not be able to use the outgoing owners' stock of invoices. However, with their permission, it is possible to use their invoice design and layout.

We found a printer local to the hotel and arranged for them to print invoices using the hotel's existing design but including our details. We had enough printed to last six months. This gave us time to work on a new design for our marketing. The invoices were delivered to the hotel a couple of days before our arrival.

Registering for VAT

If you are VAT registered for your current business you must make contact with HM Customs and Excise and inform them of your plans.

We had our event management company VAT registered and planned to continue with this in tandem with the hotel business. We have kept the same VAT registration number and simply added the hotel to the event business. This was a straightforward exercise and involved just one phone call.

If you are planning to register for VAT contact HM and Customs and Excise and they will talk you through the options. As a hotel we pay VAT quarterly at a flat rate of 8.5% of turnover. (This rises to 9.5% in year two.) Many of our purchases for the hotel do not attract VAT and the flat rate scheme saves us time and money.

Taking over the website

If your hotel has a website this should be included as part of the overall sale. It will be of no use to the outgoing owners and is an essential part of your marketing. You must arrange to take this over so that it continues to operate when you arrive. You may not like the design or layout that much but this is something you can change when you have more time.

You will need to contact the web host who might also be the web designer. The web URL will be registered and you should contact the relevant registration company to let them know when you will be taking over. They will need authorisation from the owners in writing to allow the URL to be transferred to you. You may also have to pay the hotel owners for any period that they have already paid for.

Marketing considerations

It is difficult to even begin to plan for a new marketing design before you have run the hotel for a few weeks. You may be happy with the existing design. If the occupancy levels are high the design will have played a part in the hotel's success. A new design for hotel brochures, business cards, letterheads and any information given to guests can wait until you know exactly what you want.

Notifying suppliers

Any company supplying the hotel should be made aware of the date of your arrival. Local companies supplying food, laundry, newspapers and sundry supplies should be informed by the owners. You should also make contact with them just as an introduction and to reassure them that you will require their services. There is no point in changing suppliers ahead of your move. You can decide if they measure up once you have worked with them.

The other key suppliers are the gas, electricity and water companies, the cable TV and telephone providers and your local council. A simple telephone call is all it takes to confirm your details and to check prices. Again, you can decide when you are in situ whether any of these need to change.

Last but not least – taking care of yourselves

Your own personal well-being is important. Moving home is a stressful time and starting a new business is difficult, even if you have run a hotel or your own business before.

> We made sure that we had plenty of sleep and ate properly. We did have leaving parties with our friends though we arranged these well in advance of our departure. The key to limiting the stress of the move is to be well organised and be in possession of as much information about your hotel and its location before you move.

Making the move – the big day

Communication is the key to a successful moving day. Keeping in touch with your solicitor, estate agent, removal firm and the companies supplying services is essential. Do not assume that everyone is as on the ball as you. It will not upset anyone if you approach each party at least a couple of times to check on progress. Even if it does upset them you will have relative peace of mind.

To demonstrate what can happen on such a momentous day, the following describes what happened to us.

All packed and ready to go . . .

Our removal firm arrived at 8.00 a.m. We had packed everything ready to move over the previous two weeks and we were ready for them. By 11 a.m. they had completed the removal of all of our worldly goods and wanted to make tracks for Gloucestershire. We were happy to let them go. They said they didn't mind waiting at the other end for the deal to go through. They arrived at 1 p.m., an hour before the deal was scheduled to be finalised. So far so good.

We had placed fresh clothes, which we planned to wear on the journey, on hangers on the front of our built-in wardrobes. The removal men asked for clarification on everything they picked up saying, 'Is this to go?' Unfortunately they didn't do this for our clothes and packed them on the lorry. Before we had realised what they had done it was too late – they had departed. We were left with what we had been wearing all morning!

All of the other service providers arrived on time, mainly to install new services for the incoming owners and to read meters.

We had been promised a call from our solicitors by 2 p.m. to confirm that monies had been transferred and that we were the owners of a million pound hotel. The said call duly arrived at 1.45 p.m. It was time to leave. We had arranged for grandparents to look after the children the night before the move on a Friday, and to keep them until the Sunday.

Twenty minutes into our journey we hit heavy, stationary traffic – the M25 at its best.

Twenty minutes later the mobile telephone rang. It was our sellers' solicitors asking what was happening and why they had not received funds to confirm the purchase. We explained that we had been told that this had already taken place and that we were en route. They informed us that they had been unable to contact our solicitor who appeared to have 'gone to lunch'.

Before we could call our solicitor the telephone rang again. This time it was the removal company to say that the hotel would not give them access to offload. A relatively calm and friendly man from earlier in the day was now shouting down the phone, sounding aggressive and threatening to charge us for overtime.

Before we could make a call the mobile rang yet again. This time the sellers were complaining about the attitude of the removal men and our solicitor and asking where we were. Explaining that we had left an hour ago and were stuck in traffic and that our solicitor had said the deal had gone through did not calm matters.

A call to our solicitor, who was clearly not out to lunch, confirmed that the deal had been confirmed and that the sellers' solicitors had been informed immediately by fax. We called the sellers' solicitors but found that they were still not aware that the transaction had taken place. They threatened that if they did not receive notification within 20 minutes it would be too late for funds to be released to complete the deal.

We then called the removal man and he was even more annoyed than before. He was still being refused access. We called the sellers and asked them to let the removal people in and stated that as far as we were concerned everything had already been confirmed and that their solicitors had their wires crossed. After a lengthy conversation it was agreed to allow the removal company to start offloading but on the understanding that it was at our risk.

The sellers' solicitors called again to say that they had now received instructions and all was well. It was now 3 p.m. and we still had over 90 miles to travel. The traffic had subsided. At 3.30 p.m. the removal company called to say they had finished and that they would be sending us a bill for overtime! Needless to say we didn't pay them anything extra.

We arrived at 4.30 p.m. to find that much of our garden furniture had been 'dumped' on the hotel lawn and the rest of our belongings had been 'placed' on the living room floor of our house. It was a baking hot day with the temperature hovering around 27°C.

The outgoing owners had become quite hostile and seemed agitated that we had kept them waiting for so long. They had mentioned on the telephone that they were travelling to Scotland and had a lengthy journey ahead of them, but they were annoyed because they seemed to think that we had promised to be with them by 2 p.m. We did not and could not have made such a promise. They handed over the keys and were gone within 15 minutes of our arrival.

Throughout the day we remained calm and did not raise our voices or lose our tempers. Doing so would not have been constructive and could well have added to the tension.

We had three couples checking in that afternoon and had no indication of the time they were expected. (To this day we always ask weekend guests for an estimated time of arrival as this helps plan our own weekend.)

We set about tackling the mountain of garden furniture. We were concerned that this would not make a good impression on our guests. It took over an hour to move this out of sight to our barn at the back of the property. The house was in chaos and it took several hours to introduce our furniture to the appropriate rooms. We had labelled every box in the hope that the removal firm would catch on to this and at least make an attempt to place the boxes in the right rooms.

We hadn't had any time to think about ourselves or notice the impact of making such a big change to our lives. At 6.30 p.m. our first guests arrived. They were not aware that we were new owners or of the type of day that we had had. We retired to bed at 11.30 p.m. totally exhausted. Sleeping did not come easy. Although I had checked the contents of the fridge before going to bed to ensure that there were sufficient supplies for the following morning's breakfasts, this played heavily on my mind and eventually after an hour of worry I left the comfort of my bed to visit the hotel kitchen, just to make one final check!

Even with all of our pre-planning the day did not pass as smoothly as we had hoped. It is difficult to legislate for other people and the way that they respond – after all, they were not privy to our situation or the traffic which had held us up. That said, had we not planned everything so meticulously we may well have encountered even bigger problems and our first guests could have been left waiting at the hotel front door!

6
Preparation is the key

Are you ready to run a new business?

Remaining calm under pressure is a major attribute to possess. In the hotel industry, and in particular the small hotel sector, anything can happen – and often does, usually with no advanced warning. What actually transpires is mostly unavoidable and it is not always possible to foresee what lies ahead.

Every day presents a new challenge. It is how you react to this that will determine the outcome and how much sleep you lose as a result.

Preparing for emergencies

You don't have to be a jack of all trades. If you are such a person then you have a distinct advantage. If not, then you will need to know a man – or woman – that is. We have a contact for most of the major areas of the hotel that can and do go wrong. We have a local electrician, a plumber, a heating engineer and a painter and decorator, all available within a reasonable time frame.

Hotel owners are solely responsible for everything that happens within their hotel, every day of every week. You must be in control and be thinking and planning ahead. You must be able to react calmly when a problem occurs. You must find solutions for these problems. Reacting quickly is not always possible. It often pays to take your time to consider what action to take, discuss the matter and if relevant talk to your staff. People that have worked in the hotel for some time can quite often provide the answer: in many cases they will have encountered the problem before. If the solution isn't clear and there is no immediate need to find a resolution, take a couple of days to consider all of your options. In some cases doing nothing results in the problem solving itself.

There are of course many things that will need your instant attention. These are usually obvious and will have a direct effect on the daily running of the hotel. This might involve something straightforward such as a blown light bulb or fuse. It may be a dripping tap or a radiator that isn't heating up. It could be of a more serious nature such as the central heating not working or the gas cooker malfunctioning. It sounds easy to say but the best advice is not to panic. If you have a support infrastructure most of the people on call will be available as soon as you need them.

A bed in need

We had one of our guests break a bed. They were on the heavy side and two of the bed's legs gave way. It was not possible to make good, as the damage was significant. We had new guests arriving that evening and they had specifically requested that room. So what would you do? As a hotel owner you will receive information by e-mail and through the post every day from companies wanting to supply you with one thing or another. Even if you are not interested in the product or service at the time of receipt, it is best to keep hold of the information if it refers to an item that might be of use one day. We keep this information and when the bed broke we had the details of several companies supplying new and used beds specifically for hotels. Within an hour we had purchased a new bed and by 2 p.m. it had been delivered, in plenty of time for the new guests to enjoy it.

This is just a very simple example of the type of problem you will face. The solution was fairly straightforward. The key is not to panic, but be organised and logical in your thinking. Weigh up all of your options and take the action that you decide will be of the most benefit to the hotel. You might not make the right decision. If you do not then you must learn from it and apply your knowledge next time round. If you can do this successfully you will be on the road to becoming a hotelier and will begin to enjoy yourselves.

Sticking to a daily routine

We have found that sticking to a daily routine suits us best. There are certain jobs to do that need to be carried out every day. Some need your attention just once a week or on a monthly basis. Keeping to your schedule ensures that you organise yourselves in the most effective way and will keep the hotel running smoothly.

It will become obvious to you which tasks are unavoidable and which take priority. We make a list of the daily tasks and add to these each day if something else crops up that needs our attention. We start each day with a full list and cross each task off as we go. There is satisfaction in seeing the list reduce as each job is completed. It also gives you an indication of the time involved and will give you an instant picture of how much longer you need to complete the list. It also acts as a timely reminder, specifically when the task is of importance.

It will eventually become obvious to you what needs to be done every day and you will form your own list, either in your head or on paper. We could probably function without a list but feel it would be dangerous to abandon it just in case we forget something.

Learning new tricks

If you are organised and have experience of running your own business this will be more than an asset to you. It is never too late to learn new tricks and certainly the hotel industry does throw up new challenges every day.

You must be organised and have planned your new venture well in advance of when you are due to begin. This will give you a head start. You will have to learn quickly. There is no better way of learning than actually doing, and you will be in a situation where you have to use your judgement all of the time and apply this to every situation.

If you can apply your knowledge and previous business skills to running a hotel you will be surprised at how often this applies to the situation you find yourselves in. We have had 20 years of practice at customer service and it was the most enjoyable aspect of the work we were involved with. Our experience included marketing, project management, credit management, sales, event organising and accountancy. It also included hair dressing. All of these skills are relevant to the hospitality industry.

Enjoying the challenge

If you enjoy a challenge and are not frightened of hard work you will do well. If you enjoy meeting people and have the ability to make small talk with new customers and be polite and courteous to even the most obnoxious customers, you will do well. If you take pride in your hotel and present the best possible customer service, 24 hours a day, you will enjoy being a hotelier.

Don't make the mistake of modelling yourself on Basil Fawlty or consider renaming your hotel 'Fawlty Towers'. It will be tempting and in many circumstances you will hear Basil's voice shouting inside your head. Leave him in there. He has no place in your world if you want satisfied customers that come back week after week. However, it doesn't mean that you don't have to think like him! You can say whatever you like to customers, suppliers and staff in your head, as long as you are outwardly polite and friendly at all times.

You must continually ask yourselves whether you really do want to own and run a hotel and discuss this at every opportunity.

What nobody will tell you!

The people you are buying from will not tell you what they really think about running a hotel, unless of course they are deliriously happy 100% of the time. They will think differently depending on the time of year or how they felt when they got up that morning.

> **The occasional doubt**
>
> Most of the time we feel happy that we made the change. Quite often, at least once a week to start with but now just once or twice a month, we have severe doubts. These doubts include whether we would have been better off financially if we had stayed where we were and the fact that we have very little social time and no time for a holiday. We sometimes discuss selling up and using the profit we have made so far on buying a house and not having a mortgage. We have decided that it is healthy to continually question our existence and it is definitely a good idea to continuously monitor progress.

Each hotelier will have a different outlook and a different reason for doing what they are doing. We didn't want to continue in the same routine for another 20 years. We didn't want to reach retirement regretting that we had never taken a chance or challenged ourselves just the once. The desire to be your own boss, we believe, is in everyone. Certainly it was a major factor in our decision.

Some hoteliers have sufficient finance available not to have a large mortgage. When we visited one hotel for the first time for a viewing, the owners told us that they chose when to work and when to have time off. They appeared to be in total control of their lives. They said that they took regular holidays and employed a temporary manager to run the hotel while they were sunning themselves.

Reading between the lines we realised that they had to work harder than ever just to make ends meet. They had opened their restaurant to non-residents and their bar to the public. The hotel was quite run down – we estimated that it needed at least £50,000 in refurbishments to knock it into shape – and their occupancy levels and turnover were poor.

Time for time off?

Having time off when you first start out is a luxury. We took too many weekends off in our first few months and were satisfied with the weekday trade. Paying interest only on the mortgage made working every day less of a priority. The stress of moving and beginning a totally new business added to the desire to take a few days off here and there.

We know of other hotel owners who have sufficient finance available, i.e. their own money, to enable them to run the hotel more as a hobby than a business. They take most weekends off and have several holidays a year. Back to the real world!

Making a total commitment

Owning and running a hotel to a high standard involves your total commitment. Being open seven days a week and not turning anyone away is essential if you are to make the business a success. Once you feel comfortable that you have control of your cash flow, have regular and sustainable occupancy and have saved money for that rainy day, *then* you can consider taking a weekend off now and again.

It takes approximately three years before you realise any profit from your investment personally. That's not to say you will not be making a profit. Any profit that we make is used on the business for improvements or just to keep up with the everyday expenses. We stay open every day and very rarely take time off. We do have the odd day or half day off when we have no bookings. We decided that if we were to make a success of the hotel we must encourage as much custom as possible.

A weekend off . . .

In 2007 from May to October we took only one weekend off. We were open and busy every weekend and full during the week. We believe that satisfied customers are the best form of marketing, and the least expensive. Our investment in the time spent working during this period ensured a substantial increase in our occupancy levels and much improved forward bookings for 2008. This added to the overall value of the business in terms of the price of the bricks and mortar and goodwill. Our profit is in increasing the value of the hotel for when we eventually come to sell.

Staying on top of cash flow

Running a hotel is hard work. If you have never run a hotel before or owned a business, the learning curve is as steep as it can get. Success is not guaranteed. You can only pay the bills if you have regular paying customers. Cash flow is not that straightforward. I had experience of accounting and cash flow when I worked as an assistant accountant for five years with an insurance broker. I dealt with hundreds of thousands of pounds on a daily basis. Cash flow was routine. Banking each day involved tens of thousands of pounds received from new customers and predominantly policy renewals. Most of the time I knew in advance how much money I would have to bank.

With a hotel, on the other hand, while you know how much business to expect from the bookings you receive, it is the empty rooms and not knowing whether you will be able to fill them that causes uncertainty and makes cash flow more difficult. Equally, if you have customers who have stayed for several days and only settle their bill on departure, you have to pay close attention to when you will be in a position to pay suppliers. If you have several customers all staying for a week the problem is heightened.

Putting the hotel first

If you own your hotel it will take several months before you become accustomed to everyday life. It is a big responsibility. You are always on call and must be available day and night. You must attend to your customers when they call upon you for something. Whatever they ask of you, you must be polite and courteous.

You will not have as much time for your friends or family and will, in most instances, have to put the hotel first. Your social or leisure time will be built around the hotel. When you find yourself making a decision on whether you have time for a personal engagement, you will have to consider if this fits with what is happening in the hotel. However, hotel life does become easier in time.

Preparing for the unexpected

If you are to be in a position to react successfully to the unexpected then routine is a key weapon in your armoury. Experience is also vital. Something different happens most days and you will not always know how to overcome a problem. If the dilemma requires more than 30 minutes of your time it will impact on the rest of your day. Any more than 30 minutes and you might find that you have to reschedule your entire day.

Dealing with the unexpected

If you have a routine and a schedule to follow this will free up time for you to deal with the unexpected. If you are not experienced at DIY, for example, fixing a lock on a bedroom door will take you longer than if you have completed this task before. If you take an hour longer than anticipated attending to the kitchen because you suddenly decided that the oven needed cleaning after the grill started to billow smoke, this will hold you up for the rest of the morning. If you have a regular schedule for all of the daily tasks that require your attention, you will find that the unexpected happens less, and when it does happen you will have more time to deal with it.

After about a year you will have experienced most things that can happen. You will be better equipped to cope and the unexpected will no longer be a surprise to you. It will in effect no longer be the unexpected.

Setting up a routine

Routine also enables you to complete the more mundane tasks efficiently and makes them less boring. Cleaning is a laborious duty and one that you have to do every day whether you feel like it or not. Following the same routine will ensure that the task is completed quickly and effectively. The time it takes to set up for breakfast each morning can be improved by following the same routine each day. You will find your own way of doing everything. We have found that we can cut the time it takes for each task by planning and organising our routine. It does sound boring but we have saved hours by analysing the way we approach each task and following it to the letter. This then frees us up to undertake other disciplines or to have some free time.

Employing staff

We found that some of the staff we inherited from the previous owners had, for one reason or another, become bored with the job and needed to move on. We recognised this reasonably quickly.

It is noticeable when a member of your staff is not performing at their best. They take longer tea breaks than normal and can often be found standing talking or sitting on a bed having an unscheduled break. By law, part-time staff that work for four hours a day or less are not actually entitled to a tea break. It is sensible though to make them have some time off. Cleaning rooms, for example, is strenuous and the age of your cleaning staff may play a part in this too. If you want to get the best possible result your staff will need some time during their shift to recharge their batteries.

If you inherit contracted staff you are not legally allowed to terminate their contract before you take over. This applies to part-time and full-time staff.

Doing it yourself

Employing people is never easy. You will find that you will spend longer cleaning a room than the cleaner you pay to do the job. When our cleaner is not working we undertake the cleaning ourselves. We spend 20 to 30 minutes longer in a room than our cleaner does. We attribute this to the fact that it is our hotel and we find it impossible to clean a room without spring-cleaning it entirely. Our cleaners do an excellent job and we are very happy with the end result, but they have limited time to spend on each room as they only work for four hours a day.

The staff you inherit will have a specific way of performing their duties. They will have discovered the most effective formula for their job. They may have been instructed or trained by the previous owners. This will not necessarily follow the way in which you would like to see things performed. Do not ask them to make changes to the way they work straightaway. Observe how they operate and make suggestions rather than demands. You do not want to upset your staff as soon as you arrive.

Working out staffing numbers

The number of staff you employ will depend largely on how much work you are prepared to undertake yourselves. If you are a couple and do not have a young family, you will most probably both be working in the hotel full time. If this is the case you will need fewer staff.

Before you take over the business you should decide which jobs you feel will suit you best and which you would prefer to employ someone else to do. You can always change this once you have run the hotel for a few weeks.

If one of you is looking after children full or part time, or you plan that one of you will continue in alternative employment, you will not both be able to work full time in the hotel and as such will need to divide up the most critical work between you.

Our staff

We run a ten-bedroom hotel. During the week we have between ten and twelve guests each day. At weekends we can cater for up to 20 guests. We have seven staff working for us: three are contracted, the rest students. Of the three contracted staff, one is our housekeeper, one a cleaner and the other a waitress. The contracted staff work Monday to Friday. We have two evening receptionists who work alternate days, Monday to Thursday. The other two are waitresses and work on Saturday and Sunday and during school holidays.

We do not both work in the hotel as we have a young family. Our level of staffing ensures that the hotel runs smoothly and we have cover if a member of staff is off sick or on holiday.

If you are both running your hotel you will not require this level of staff. If you do not want to clean the rooms yourselves you will need two cleaners. Cleaning ten rooms on your own is extremely tiring. On your own this takes most of the day, with two of you involved it takes four to five hours. If the work is to be carried out to a reasonable standard you have to allocate sufficient time to thoroughly clean each room.

Getting staff levels right

When we first started we were overstaffed. On weekdays we had a breakfast cook and two waitresses. Two people are able to cope with up to 16 guests for breakfast. It is preferable, however, and less stressful to have three kitchen staff when you have 14 or more guests. It is possible to run the kitchen with just one person cooking and waiting on ten guests. We have had several mornings when our waitress was unable to work and we did not have time to find a replacement. It is not something we care to repeat too often!

Staffing in the kitchen

The kitchen is a crucial place and having the right mix of people working for you at breakfast time is essential. Finding people to start early in the day is a problem. Our day starts in the kitchen at 6.25 a.m. and our waitress arrives at 6.45 a.m. Having local people work for you is therefore a bonus, and ensures they have an easy journey to work and do not have to set out too early.

Staff must be cheerful when waiting on tables, even if the customer is grumpy or in a bad mood. The last thing your guests need first thing in the morning is a miserable waiter or waitress. The success of your business is dependent on your reputation and the highest standard of customer service will result in customers returning time and again. Make sure that your waiting staff know this and observe how they behave when talking to your guests. The best way of judging if they are suitable is to ask your guests when they are checking out.

If you plan to run the kitchen yourselves and do all of the cooking but have no experience you need to practise before you take over. If you already have experience it will take time to become accustomed to your working environment and it will help greatly if you have waiting staff that are familiar with the layout of the kitchen.

In at the deep end

Our cook had a broken arm when we arrived. She worked in a supervisory capacity and helped us to find our feet. Unfortunately we parted company with her after six months and decided not to employ a replacement. I personally had very little experience of running a kitchen, let alone catering for up to 20 guests. Initially I worked at breakfast and had the task of cooking eggs to order. I picked up enough tips in the first six months to feel confident to take over the cooking when the cook left.

Staffing reception

Our evening reception staff are students. One is taking a gap year and the other studying law. They are both 19 years of age. They are cheerful and presentable and our guests frequently comment on how friendly and personable they are.

Eighty per cent of our business guests are men. Having someone other than yourself at reception is a welcome change for your customers.

> **Evening receptionist**
>
> Employing an evening receptionist is a luxury as we could run the reception ourselves. However, as we do not live on the hotel premises, if we are called upon for service at any time during the evening, we have to leave the comfort of our home to attend the hotel. Having a receptionist on site allows us to take each weekday evening off and have some time for ourselves. The reception is manned from 7 p.m. to 11 p.m. on weekdays and we look after the reception at weekends. The receptionists are responsible for closing the hotel and bar at the end of the day so we do not have to work again until the next morning.

Replacing staff who are leaving

When an existing member of your staff decides to leave, if they are contracted they will have to give you notice. This gives you time to look for a replacement. Our housekeeper has worked for us for over a year and our cleaner has been working at the hotel for over two years. Our waiting and kitchen personnel have caused us the biggest headaches when it comes to replacements. Finding people to work first thing in the morning is not easy.

> **Finding new staff**
>
> Initially, when someone left, we found an immediate solution by canvassing our staff. In every case they were able to suggest a friend or relative. This is the least expensive recruitment method, as it does not involve advertising or using an agency. Additionally, you have less worry when you employ someone known to your staff as they are more likely to be reliable and will not want to let you down.
>
> Employing younger staff, of the teenage variety, is likely to be a short-term solution. If they are weekend or just casual labour the likelihood of them finding a full-time job in time is high. Our younger workforce have mostly stayed with us for a few months and have then started upon a career. It is not possible to do much to counter this as they will have their own ambitions and you will not be able to afford to offer them a full-time position.

Just recently we have exhausted our supply of friends and relatives and have had to advertise for a couple of positions. To attract local people you need to ask the local contacts that you have. If you have made friends with other local businesses or are on friendly terms with your suppliers they are a good starting point. You may also find that the local supermarket or newsagents have a notice board advertising local services.

We recently placed a small ad for a cleaner in one issue of our local weekly newspaper and did not have a single reply. It cost us £80. The same advertisement placed for two weeks in the wool shop in our high street led to three enquiries.

We filled one of our vacancies from this advertisement. A few weeks later our waitress announced she was leaving us for a full-time position in a local high street shop. As her new position involved a 9 a.m. start time and more money we had no alternative but to look for a new waitress.

We turned to the local job centre. Within minutes of our call to them they had promoted our vacancy online and within the nearby job centre. Over the course of the next few days we received eight enquiries and found a suitable replacement. While we do have the details of several employment agencies, and temporary staff bureaus, the job centre was the most cost-effective. It was free and accessible online within seconds!

Employing teenagers

You should note that if you employ teenagers there are rules governing the hours they may work. You must apply for an 'Employment Permit' for all children of compulsory school age. The department concerned with children and young people at your local county council will be able to supply you with the correct information. The Children and Young Persons Act 1933 as amended applies. One of the main regulations dictates that no child may be employed for more than four continuous hours without a rest break of one hour or more.

Valuing your staff

We value our staff highly. Without them our lives would be nigh on impossible. We have discussed at length not having staff other than the bare minimum.

Having had experience of all of the daily tasks required, we decided that if we had no staff helping us, we would be working without a break from dusk to dawn. It is possible to do this but you would achieve burn out very quickly and would not have time for anything other than cooking and cleaning. It is important that when guests arrive you are on the top of your form and that you are ready to welcome them and make them feel comfortable. You will not be able to do this if you are worn out.

We were blasé about running a hotel. Before we knew what was actually involved we believed that the people we employed would do all of the work. We would be left to enjoy looking after the guests and promoting the hotel – in essence having time to ourselves and time to build up business. Our staff work hard and are conscientious. They make a huge contribution to our success. As such we try to make their working lives as enjoyable as we can. We do not follow them around and make comments if they have forgotten to do something or we feel that they could do better. We encourage and praise them. If we find something not to our liking we try to find a way in which to let them know about this without confrontation and causing bad feeling.

By all means let the people working for you know what is required of them, and if they forget to do something a simple reminder is all that is needed. If you respect them and treat them well, they will repay you with efficiency and loyalty. Several of our workforce have booked rooms for family and have recommended us to friends.

Avoiding discrimination

We do not discriminate on age or sex. Each gender and each age group have their good and bad sides. We have a 74-year-old lady working for us, and a 60-year-old lady. We have 15- and 17-year-old teenagers working weekends and several 19- to 21-year-olds have worked for us during our time here. We also have a 40-year-old and a 45-year-old working for us. We have enjoyed working with all of them. One or two have come and gone within a short space of time. Many have stayed for more than a year. We are resigned to having a continual turnover and have accepted this as par for the course.

What you need to know about suppliers

If you are taking over a successful business, the companies that supply the hotel will have played a part in this success. You should make contact with the key suppliers before you take over. They will be looking for your assurance that you will not be discontinuing their service. Even if you have other suppliers waiting in the wings it is prudent not to upset the apple cart before you have experienced what they have to offer first hand.

Finding out about suppliers

You should question the people you are buying the hotel from on which suppliers they use and ask them directly what type of service they have enjoyed. If they are willing to tell you, you should find out what they have told their suppliers about you and whether you plan to continue to work with them.

There are many types of companies that supply hotels. Just one or two may have supplied your hotel or the previous owners may have sourced their supplies from far and wide. You must establish the different supplies that come into the hotel on a regular basis before you take over, and find out why the previous owners used each particular company.

By calling each key supplier you immediately establish a relationship. From the conversation you have with them, you will be able to make an initial judgement on whether the supplier will be a useful contact for you in the future. It is important to let them know the date that you will be arriving and, if you wish to continue working with them, when they will next deliver supplies to you.

If an outside laundry contractor services your hotel, you may find that they have a long-term agreement with the hotel and that this is to be carried over to any new owners. This may be true of other suppliers.

Food supplies may well have been sourced locally. There are countless small businesses working in the food industry and they provide a cost-effective and environmentally friendly alternative to some of the bigger stores. They may also

121

deliver to you and this saves valuable time. All you will need to do is make a telephone call to place an order.

Paying suppliers

Your key suppliers will expect to be paid on time and in some cases on delivery. This is a must if you are to rely on them.

If the previous owners have already shopped around for the best deal and the best quality, there is little point in revisiting this exercise as soon as you arrive. If the guests are happy with the service they receive and repeat business is strong, the formula will need nothing more than a slight adjustment here and there.

If you are not happy with a supplier, once you have worked with the existing one for a while you can make the change then. When you first start out it is advisable to keep as much as you can the way it was before you arrived. This ensures continuity and will avoid you making any costly mistakes.

Investigating alternatives

Having said all this, it is prudent to investigate all possible alternatives. You can do this at any time, but you will find that it is best to do so as soon as you feel comfortable that you know what your customers expect and you have decided what you would like to change. It is time-consuming and risky finding new suppliers. Once you have met other local businesses it may also be possible to ask for advice and recommendations.

Sorting the laundry

We have a laundry company supplying us. They collect and deliver every Tuesday and Friday. When we first arrived we inherited the hotel linen stock. The previous owners had purchased a good quality supply sufficient to withstand constant use for a couple of years. We pay between £500 and £1,000 per month depending on occupancy.

After a year we investigated the cost of contract laundry. Several local laundry companies approached us during our first year. We were reasonably satisfied with our supplier and they did not let us down at any stage. This is an important factor. We also received approaches from a washing and drying machine supplier who tried to convince us that we could save vast sums if we washed our own laundry.

We know of some hotels that clean their own laundry. An industrial washer and dryer can cost as little as £35 per week. On the third approach by the same company we were even offered a complete supply of new laundry if we agreed to hire their machines on contract. They even offered to refit our cellar or build a laundry room in our grounds!

If you compare the cost of this to using an outside laundry it is a tempting offer. However, we do not wish to spend several hours a day washing, drying and ironing and would not contemplate this even if it were offered as a free service. You have to decide if you value your time more. Two hours a day spent on laundry could be used more effectively.

The people we took over from laundered some of their own table linen so we started out doing the same. On average we spent an hour a day on this. As an experiment we gave this up and placed all of our linen in the hands of our laundry service which added £25 per month to our laundry bill. We decided to continue to use our supplier for this as we felt that the extra cost represented good value considering the time we saved by not laundering the linen ourselves.

We investigated contract cleaning. We received two quotes for the supply of linen and weekly laundry services. Some of our laundry was in need of replacement and we had already started to replace some of the towels and sheets. Contract cleaning involves the laundry service supplying all of your linen and laundry and replacing any worn or damaged items as part of the service.

As an introduction, one of the companies offered us a monthly charge, guaranteed for two years. This undercut our existing supplier. At the same time our supplier had indicated that they were considering increasing their charges by 5%. The new company only delivered once a week and we felt that this might leave us short of laundry at our busiest times. We also wanted to be fair to our supplier, as they had given a satisfactory service. We explained the offer we had received and that we had decided we needed to cut the cost of our laundry, as we needed to renew some of our stock. Our supplier agreed to offer us a contract hire service without increasing their costs guaranteed for two years. Had they not done so we would have more than likely changed supplier.

Contract hire works well for us. It allows us to reject any worn or damaged stock at any time. This maintains our standards.

We shop for food supplies on a Monday and Thursday. We often top this up with minor purchases every day. Luckily we have a wide choice of major supermarket chains within a five-mile radius of the hotel. Additionally we have many small local shops within walking distance. If we chose to, we could source all of our food shopping from the local smaller stores. This of course would be much more expensive.

When we first arrived we shopped at just one supermarket. We now buy supplies from two as this saves money. We took our time and followed our predecessors' choices for several months. They informed us that they had tried and tested all of the food that they offered to guests and this had determined where they shopped.

Sourcing your supplies

We always look for quality. We place this ahead of price. A combination of both helps us to maintain the service that we offer. If you have sufficient budget and enjoy above average turnover you will already be sourcing your supplies in this way. You may even be in a position not to consider price and decide on the best quality at all times. With a small hotel your desire to provide the highest quality is tempered by a modest turnover and equally modest profit margin. You need to find the middle ground. Guests will only stay with you once if they receive poor service of any kind.

You should ask why supplies are purchased from certain stores and decide whether this is for the right reason. If you are a bed-and-breakfast hotel the breakfast ingredients are very easy to decide upon. If you buy a hotel offering full or half board you will be making decisions on your menu on a regular basis. In this instance you will have to decide which shops offer the best quality and the best value. Cost is of course an issue and your budget will determine which direction you go in. The mix of quality and cost will always be a consideration.

Food and laundry are our two biggest budget items apart from the mortgage. We pay a great deal of attention to this and constantly analyse and discuss the situation, not only together but also with our suppliers and with our staff.

Many of the other supplies that you will need may be ordered over the telephone or online and delivered to you. You could apply this to everything if you wanted to.

Regular deliveries

Daily

◆ *Newspapers*. We receive the *Daily Mail* and *The Times* and our guests have never asked for any alternatives. Our local newsagent is a five-minute walk away and we pay the bill monthly and on time. The bill is also delivered. The monthly cost is, on average, £58 and includes the Sunday papers.

Weekly

◆ *Bacon*. We order four 5lb packs per week or whenever we run low. This is delivered by a local farm. We inherited this supplier and it was immediately obvious that the quality of the meat supplied was exceptional. We taste all of the food we give to guests almost every day and the bacon receives countless compliments. We currently pay £32.87 per delivery.

◆ *Eggs*. Again, we source these locally and they are delivered. We pay £4.35 for five dozen eggs. We call our supplier and they arrive next day. If we call them before 8 a.m. they deliver on the same day.

Every other week

◆ *Croissants*. These are delivered frozen and stored in our freezer. They take 15 minutes to bake in the oven. We purchase a pack of 100 at a cost of £30.32.

Initially we also purchased part-baked bread rolls from the same supplier. These were not popular with our guests and we discontinued them once we had become weary of throwing most of them away each day.

Monthly or less

◆ *Water.* We place a 330ml glass bottle of still water in each room. We include two bottles for double occupancy. This is complimentary. The supplier is a local specialist company and the bottles are branded.

If you are wondering why we do not charge for this you should think back to when you last stayed in a hotel. Did you have access to a glass of water whenever you needed a drink? Chances are you didn't. We feel that this sets us apart from our competitors. Yes, it is an expense and people in this day and age do not expect it. We decided to continue with this practice and have not once considered cutting this.

Water on tap?

Having spent many nights in some of the top hotels it always annoyed me if I needed a glass of water and had to pay for it from a mini bar, if in fact the room had such a thing.

On our wedding day we stayed in a small hotel similar to ours. On departure to the ceremony I asked for a glass of water. It was a hot day and my mouth was dry. The owner was serving behind the bar and he charged me £1.35 for a glass of tap water.

We often have guests ask to pay for a bottle of water they have used in their room. We pay 29 pence per bottle.

The previous owners placed either sparkling or still water, or both, in each room. We discontinued using sparkling water a month into our ownership. Very few guests drink sparkling water and in 18 months not one guest has asked for it. The cost for each option is the same.

Toiletries

The company that supplies us insists on payment at the time of order. We have researched other suppliers and found that they all offer a similar service and while cost savings can be made if you switch from company to company, most charge a similar rate. While it is possible to sacrifice quality to save cost, we find that our guests expect a certain quality and as such they would notice any slight change. Your budget will decide and you will have a personal preference.

Investigating wholesalers

We investigated wholesale stores before we started and compared the cost and breadth of provisions available in each. We also considered their location and how long a trip to the wholesalers would take.

We visit the wholesaler once every six weeks although they do deliver if you choose this option. We prefer to see what we are buying and have the opportunity to impulse buy. Quite often we find that we have forgotten to include an item on our shopping list and a visit to the store jogs our memory. This is not possible if you have goods delivered.

We have an account with our wholesalers and have found that they suit our needs precisely. If they do not stock something there are plenty of other places to fill any gaps.

We also use the wholesaler to purchase various provisions including the following:
- A4 paper
- anti-bacterial hand wash
- anti-bacterial surface cleaner
- apple juice
- bathroom/toilet cleaner
- breakfast cereals
- biscuits for guest bedrooms

- coffee
- coffee sticks for guest bedrooms
- dishwasher tabs
- DL envelopes
- drinking chocolate sachets for guest bedrooms
- dusters
- furniture polish
- HP sauce
- J cloths
- ketchup
- kitchen rolls
- marmalade
- milk/cream (long-life) for guest bedrooms
- muesli
- orange juice
- paper napkins (3 ply)
- pedal bin liners
- strawberry jam
- sweets for reception area
- tea bags
- tissues
- toilet cleaner
- toilet rolls
- tropical fruit juice
- washing-up liquid.

We also purchase alcohol and soft drinks for our bar.

The bill on average comes to £350 every six weeks. The provisions we purchase are essential items. The wholesaler stocks most brands and has a butchery and grocery section. From time to time we have also purchased other items such as kitchen utensils, stationery, light bulbs, toiletries, glassware and crockery.

Other offers

On a daily basis we receive post and e-mail offers from a host of different companies trying to sell us their wares. We keep the details of most of the mail we receive and in particular anything that is of specific interest. We also take at least one telephone call per day and once or twice a week we welcome a door-to-door sales rep. In a typical week we are offered: a bathroom repair service, cheaper electricity, bedroom furniture, other hotels for sale, toiletries, electrical goods, lounge furniture, staff uniforms and crockery.

While this is annoying you never know when the need for one of these items will arise. If you keep all of the more interesting details for future reference you will have little trouble in finding a supplier when you need one.

Cleaning the windows

Once a month we have a window cleaner visit. He cleans all of the outside windows one month, and cleans inside and out every other month. The cost is £43.90 for the outside and £91.84 for inside and out. We also have an agreement with our window cleaner to cover accidental damage. For any glass that he accidentally breaks we share the replacement cost between us. We came to this agreement because health and safety dictates that the window cleaner must use an extension pole to clean the second- and top-floor windows. He has on occasion broken a pane of glass using this system. Our agreement ensures that he takes greater care when cleaning and is not responsible for the complete replacement cost which we feel would be unfair.

Tending the grounds

Although the grounds of our hotel are not that substantial we do employ a gardener to cut the grass. When we first arrived we did not have time for this ourselves. From April through to October the grass is cut once a week. The gardener is here for a couple of hours and disposes of the cuttings. This saves us valuable time and the expense is bearable.

If your hotel has a garden or substantial grounds you must plan how to deal with this. Gardening is time-consuming and if you are not a keen gardener it can be very boring and also tiring. The appearance of the hotel is as important outside as it is internally. First impressions go a long way when you are trying to attract new business and to retain the old. Between March and October you will have to be in control of any garden or grounds, however big or small. This will involve at least one day a week tidying, pruning, mowing and clearing. A gardener is an expense but the cost is outweighed by the time he or she saves you.

Dealing with other suppliers

The other companies involved in your hotel include the utility and telephone suppliers, cable TV, plumber, electrician, maintenance, decorator, website host and a variety of others that you will need to call upon at one time or another.

You will find that shopping around the utility suppliers for your gas and electricity will pay dividends, though initially you will have to keep the existing supplier. Studying the terms of the contract will ensure that you are aware of what you are being charged and when you are required to give notice of termination when you decide to change. Most utility companies require three months' notice to terminate; however, this can be as much as six months. They will send you details of their new tariff a few months in advance of renewal and you need to make sure that when you receive this you are in time to cancel if you wish to do so. Shopping around will save you money. Heating and lighting a hotel, especially in the winter months, is a costly exercise.

Light fantastic!

We inherited scores of light bulbs when we moved in. They were all standard 40- and 60-watt bulbs and were replacements for the various lights throughout the hotel. Each bedroom has four or five light bulbs. Any light that has to be left on most of the day and night is linked to the emergency lighting system. We found that when we started we had to change at least one light bulb every day. If one of the hall lights blew it tripped the fuse and switched over to emergency lighting. All of the other lights in this section of the hotel turn off when this takes place. In certain bedrooms, if one bulb blew all of the power in that room was shut down, leaving the guest in darkness. Within a couple of weeks, when this became impractical we purchased long-life light bulbs. The budget dictated that we could only do this gradually. Over the course of a three-month period we replaced all of the light bulbs in the hotel. The cost for this type of bulb is reducing and if you shop around many places have special offers from time to time.

Health and safety dictates that our staircases and reception area must be lit at all times and specifically when guests or staff are on the premises.

With most utility or telephone suppliers, you really only notice them when something goes wrong or the price increases. It does take time to investigate cost-effective solutions to your needs. You can and will save hundreds of pounds if you continuously search for the best option.

Planning for your first few days

If this is your first venture into hotel ownership, the first few days and weeks after you start may well be a traumatic experience. Your new environment will offer you a different challenge almost every day. If you are a couple or partnership you must support each other and work together. You will soon find which jobs suit you best and these will become your responsibility in future months.

A hotel shared . . .

Sharing tasks effectively halves the workload and allows you to complete more duties in a shorter time span. For the first year or our ownership I worked alone in the hotel, as we had a young family not yet at school. This is now changing and we have both started to share the day-to-day management. At every stage we discuss our plans and let each other know what we would like to achieve.

Working in this way is less stressful and sharing any problem allows you to discuss and resolve key issues. It also produces ideas and these can bring new revenue streams.

Hitting the ground running

When you are planning to start work you should be prepared to hit the ground running. It is virtually impossible for the owners of the hotel to plan when the final moving date will be and they will continue to take bookings on your behalf. You will almost certainly be taking over when guests are in residence or due to arrive.

This will also depend on the type of hotel that you are buying. If you are moving in out of season you may not have any guests at all. If this is the case your budget must allow for a period when you have little or no income. If on the other hand you are moving into this type of business in high season you must be prepared to start work as soon as you arrive. The upside of this is that you will immediately benefit from the revenue that you receive. You must also be aware that if you have a guest that has stayed for a period with the outgoing owners and then with you, you will have to agree how this is accounted for. It is doubtful that your new customers will be aware of a change in ownership.

Keeping the staff and suppliers on side

It is essential that you are ready to be hoteliers from the moment you arrive. With a hotel in a tourist destination or at the seaside where you are providing full or half board, it should be possible to start before the existing owners have moved out. If they have guests enjoying full or half board you must ensure that they are catered for and this will be difficult if you arrive a few minutes before dinnertime.

In this instance your staff will play a vital role. Speaking to them before you arrive and letting them know what your expectations are will ease the pressure. If you need them on your first day make sure that you ask them to work and that you know what time they start and finish their shift. Find out what they think their duties include. You should also have been supplied with copies of any staff contracts and these will confirm job descriptions. Once you have observed your staff in action you can decide if these are relevant or if they need rewriting.

To make life easier for you and more comfortable for your guests, you should consider asking all of your staff to be available to work for you for the first few days. The first day after we arrived at our hotel we had 20 guests staying. The hotel was full. To say that we were nervous when contemplating the first morning is an understatement. We organised for two of our waitresses and our cook to work that morning. As our cook had a broken arm and was acting in a supervisory capacity I was responsible for breakfast. If you have not worked in a commercial kitchen environment before it is a daunting prospect. While we cursed the previous owners for booking in so many guests on our first day, it gave us an ideal start. We experienced what life would be like in the weeks and months to come and got our hands dirty straightaway. Eighteen months on we have managed breakfast for 20 guests on several occasions with just one waitress and myself as breakfast chef.

The stock you inherit must be sufficient to see you through the first week at least. This includes the kitchen, food, linen, bar and dining room. The staff you employ must be made aware that you want them to work for you and when they are expected to start. All suppliers must be in place and provide continuity of service. Most will continue regardless as they do not wish to lose business. However, you must not assume that this is the case.

No time for time off!

Do not plan to take any time off in the first few days – or weeks for that matter. Your new business will require your undivided attention. For your own morale arrange for one of your dearest friends or closest family to visit you a week or two after you have taken over. Arrange the visit for a day of the week when you have the least number of guests staying with you. This will give you a boost and you can enjoy showing off your new environment. If you have moved some distance you may have to accommodate them.

Aiming for a seamless takeover

You must have everything you need to run the hotel available to you from day one. This is essential if you are to convince the regular guests that you are going to maintain the hotel to the high standards they have become accustomed to or even improve them. They do not need to know straightaway whether you are a novice or an old hand. Persuading them that you are in control and that you know what you are doing is much easier if you meet all of their demands and behave in a professional manner.

You should also plan the action you need to take once you have arrived and your names are above the door. The sooner you remove any trace of the previous owners' involvement the better. You will want to see your names on the hotel website, on any letterhead and in any other relevant marketing or advertising material.

Registration forms

You will need registration forms for when guests check in. A supply of hotel brochures and a note of your tariff should be available to any potential customers or guests who ask for them.

Updating the website

The hotel website should continue online without any interruption. To achieve this you need to find out which company the URL is registered with and arrange for the URL to be transferred to your ownership. This will involve the sellers of the hotel completing a form giving their consent to the transfer which will almost certainly require a registration fee to be paid (by you).

If you are to change the design and layout of the website you can do this once you have arrived. If you have your own web designer they will most probably need access to some or all of the content of the site. You will need to know who designed the site originally and make contact with them to ask for the appropriate files.

Help from the outgoing owners

It may be possible to have the outgoing owners stay with you for the first few days to ease you in gently. If this is an option open to you it is advisable to make the most of the opportunity. There will be ample time in the future for you to make your own mark.

> We had to plan our first few days in advance knowing that we had a full hotel on our first day and that the sellers planned to leave within minutes of our arrival. If the sellers had stayed just for two or three days we are certain it would have been to our advantage.

Who you will need to contact

In addition to the existing suppliers and the hotel staff you also need to contact the relevant local authorities and emergency services. Some of the local authorities will already know about you from your premises and personal licence applications.

You will need to contact the local police and fire safety authority. It is advisable to know the location of the nearest hospital and ambulance station too. Your business insurers will want to know the distance each service is located from your hotel.

Contacting the police

When contacting the local police authority you should speak to them about the conditions of your premises and personal licences. They will be most interested in the timings of your licensable activities, i.e. the opening times of your bar if you have one. Having a friendly and open relationship with the police ensures that that they will respond to you and take you seriously if you are in need of them.

Known to the police

We registered for a local 'Hotel Watch' scheme, similar to 'Pub Watch'. Under the Data Protection and Telecommunications Acts we gave the police the authority to place our details on a computerised database and to receive automated messages from them. As a result we receive regular updates of any local developments or initiatives. Many forces have a Stronger and Safer Neighbourhood Group and most areas have Neighbourhood Watch schemes. By making initial contact with the police we are now involved with both and as a result we have a voice in what happens locally. This gives us access to useful information and we get to meet new people who eventually could provide us with custom.

Within a couple of days of moving in we invited our local police to visit us just as an introduction. We discussed the local community and our new environment. Contacting local services in this way will give you an insight into what happens in your area and what you can expect.

Contacting the fire services

The fire brigade for your area may or may not wish to visit you. It will depend on the legal requirements at the time.

Fire Certificate

Our hotel had been granted a Fire Certificate issued under the Fire Precautions Act 1971. The document is 28 pages in length and goes into every detail of fire safety. The certificate was issued in July 2003 when the hotel first opened. The layout of the hotel had been agreed with the Fire Authority and in accordance with the legal requirements. If your hotel has been issued with such a document you must read this and make yourselves aware of all of the conditions within. Even if it is 28 pages long – or more – read the entire document as it will help you to devise your own risk assessment.

Since our hotel received its Fire Certificate there have been changes. The responsibility for fire safety is now the onus of the hotel owner. When you make contact with the fire authority they will be able to confirm when your hotel was last inspected or the date of the next inspection.

Fire safety audit

Under the Regulatory Reform (Fire Safety) Order 2005 all hotels have to undergo a fire safety audit. You should ask the sellers if this has recently been carried out and, if it has, what the outcome was. If the audit uncovers problems these will undoubtedly involve a cost. Sometimes this can be substantial.

> We spoke recently with another hotel owner who had just been audited and the improvements demanded by the Fire Authority cost several hundred pounds.

Inspection

The inspector involved in the audit will require details of your fire safety procedures and this will include:

◆ a fire risk assessment;
◆ records of staff training;
◆ records of fire drills; and
◆ records of testing and maintenance of fire safety systems such as the fire alarm, fire-fighting equipment and escape lighting.

Risk rating and re-inspection

Once the audit has taken place your premises will be risk rated and placed on the re-inspection programme. You will be advised when to expect a re-inspection. We recently completed this and our next inspection is in approximately five years.

Keeping up to date

You must keep up to date with the most recent regulations and not rely on the fire authority to contact you on a regular basis. Most of the safety procedures are common sense. Access to up-to-date information on your duties is straightforward and you will find useful data on the local fire authority's website.

Contacting the Food Safety Department

As an establishment providing guests with food you must also contact the county council's Food Safety Department within Environmental Services and register your premises as a Food Business Establishment. You will be required to complete a form and will receive a visit by an environmental officer. They will discuss what is required of you and will inspect your kitchen and any other public area. Whether you just serve breakfast or also provide your guests with an evening meal will dictate how closely they keep tabs on you. You will be classed as a certain level of risk where food is concerned, and inspections will be more frequent if you are providing half or full board.

Again, most food hygiene is based on common sense and high standards of cleanliness are simple to maintain. Your recent food hygiene training will have prepared you for this and if you apply what you have learned and continue to do so over the coming years you will not upset anyone.

Setting up credit card processing

The key piece of equipment required to run a hotel is of course the credit card-processing machine. Once you have shopped around for the best possible deal on commission rates you must arrange for the machine to be delivered to the hotel. You will only be able to accept cheques or cash if this is not in place on the day you arrive.

It is possible to take over the existing owners' agreement with the supplier and for them to transfer their card processing facilities to you. This is not ideal. You will have little prospect of negotiating a preferential rate and are more likely to inherit the charges previously made.

Once you have chosen a suitable supplier you will be sent a card-processing machine ahead of your arrival. Ours was sent to the hotel in the week before we arrived. It should be a simple case of plugging the machine into the mains, connecting it to a telephone line and calling the service provider to register with them. You should also be sent a manual card machine to process payments in the event that you have a problem with the electronic version. When we took over the electronic machine malfunctioned and we had to send it back. Processing manual payments is not much fun and you have to send or take the receipt slips to the bank and pay them in.

You've arrived – what next?

On your first day you will be excited and nervous at the prospect of running your hotel. You will also at some point realise that your lives have changed completely and that you are now tied to your business for better or for worse. You will be at your guest's beck and call 24 hours a day and there is no escape from this. You will learn in time to make time for yourselves and that at certain hours of the day you can take a break without fear of being disturbed.

You will begin to meet the people you contacted prior to your arrival. You may have to call some of the authorities to remind them that you have arrived. There is little point in trying to hide from them and if you make first contact it demonstrates your willingness to comply with all legal regulations.

Making contact with any neighbours or other local businesses close by is a good starting point. The more people that you meet the more potential customers you open yourselves to. They will also be curious about you and it is an opportunity to put their minds at rest at an early stage. You will also begin to make friendships and to learn what happens in the local community. Later on these relationships may also be useful in helping you to find new staff or suppliers.

Once you are running your new business there is absolutely nothing to stop you running it your way. You do not have to copy your predecessors in every aspect of the hotel management. Be wary though – most of what they achieved will be as a result of sound business practices and should not be ignored, just adapted to suit your way of working.

Unbeknown to us before we arrived, the previous owners had made a list of everything that needed to be done each day. This started with setting up for breakfast in the morning and continued to lockdown at 11 p.m. They had itemised all tasks in chronological order. It proved to be a valuable tool over our first week. It helped us to locate the utensils in the kitchen, told us when to turn the oven and hot cupboards on and gave us full details on lighting, heating and where we could find everything that we would possibly need. We stopped using the list after three days – by then we knew pretty much all that we needed to and had begun our own routine, adapted from the lists that they had left behind.

Getting along with the staff

If you employ staff to work for you they will also be curious about you. More importantly, they will be concerned for the future. Even if you promised before you took over that their jobs are safe, human nature dictates that they will have doubts about you and their job security. When you have the chance to talk to them take the opportunity to reassure them. Ask them what they actually do, even if this is obvious. You can ask them if there is anything they would change in the hotel and if there is something that you can do for them to make their job easier. If you discussed the staff with the previous owners and they gave you a copy of contracts and job specifications these will not necessarily describe what actually happens.

Don't make any rash promises to your staff. They will not expect an immediate pay rise or a major change to their working conditions. Most will be happy to continue where they left off and that you have not made any immediate major changes to their routine. You can promise to treat them fairly, to listen to any suggestions they have and to show them that you are prepared to undertake any task to ensure the business runs smoothly. Demonstrating that you are willing to get your hands dirty and muck in sets a good example. You need to do this anyway as it is a part of that steep learning curve. If any of your key staff are off sick or on holiday you will have to clean rooms and wait on tables. As such you need to know where everything is located.

Checking the stock

If you have been left stock you should have a stock list. Check this as soon as you can. You need to find out if the list is complete and whether you need to order any item which is about to run out. Checking stock can take several hours. It can include food, alcohol, linen, cutlery, crockery, kitchen utensils, furniture, table lamps, glassware, stationery and so on. We checked the stock over the first two days so as not to impact on other tasks. Checking the stock left to you is a laborious task, although one that is totally necessary. You need to check that you have been left everything that has been promised and if you have no experience of hotel management it can also act as a guide to what you will need to order in the not to distant future.

Checking the hotel

Take a tour of the hotel as soon as you can. Inspect all of the guest bedrooms and see how you feel about owning a hotel now you are actually in charge. If you have guests yet to check in make sure that their rooms are clean and tidy and that the carpet has been vacuumed. If it is late afternoon during the winter turn on bedside lamps and close the curtains. This gives the room a cosy feel and puts guests at their ease when they enter.

Check that all the common areas are clean and tidy and that the dining room has been set for the next sitting. Take stock in the kitchen and make sure that you have the correct amount of supplies for the next few days. If the previous owners have promised to leave sufficient supplies for a few days, make sure that you have what you need and make a shopping list for when you next need to order or shop for supplies.

Paying your staff

You will need to pay your staff at some point. Initially you will have to pay them by cheque or in cash. We now pay our staff by bank transfer and conduct the transaction by online banking. Our predecessors always paid by cheque every

Friday. We found that the staff did not like this and preferred to have the money paid directly into their bank account. This is by far the most convenient way of paying wages, as it requires little effort. Your staff do not have to visit their bank or post the cheque. All you have to do is hand them their pay slip.

Paying wages online does mean that the money leaves your account on the day you arrange the payment and takes two or three days to reach the recipient. (When you first set this up it can take four days.) You will have to account for this and ensure you have sufficient funds in your account to pay your staff. The upside of this is that making online payments does not incur bank charges whereas a direct debit, cheque and even cash withdrawals do, depending on who you bank with of course.

Making sure that your staff are paid on time is vital. They will have bills to pay or might even rely on their wages to pay their mortgage or rent. We use the services of a payroll company which we found on the internet. They are inexpensive and efficient and take care of all of the paperwork. All you need to do is e-mail or call them with details of the hours worked and they return the payslips telling you how much to pay.

Checking bookings

Look through your appointments diary and check the weeks ahead. Get a feel for who has booked in and why they have booked, i.e. on holiday, on route to somewhere or on business. If you have guests staying for several days you will not receive payment until they check out and it will take three or four days for these funds to reach your bank account. You need to account for this.

Making yourself known to the bank

If you have opened a business account with a new bank invite your new account manager to pay you a visit. If you have opened one with your own bank also invite them to pay you a visit. If they are worth their salt they will contact you to arrange this. Let them know your initial plans and ask them to explain their charges to you. Most business accounts will have a period of free banking when you first open them. You should ask if it is possible to extend this beyond the agreed period. If you have just one year before bank charges apply this comes round sooner than you think. There is no harm in asking to increase this – it exhibits your desire to control costs and to maximise on your investment. However, don't be surprised when they refuse!

Reviewing your website

The hotel website will be at the cutting edge of your marketing plan. If it is not, you should make it so. Nearly everybody has access to the web. If you are booking a holiday and can see what you are booking before you make a commitment you are more likely to book. Even when potential guests call you for details they will often ask you for your web address so that they can check you out before they make a decision.

Before you arrived you will have discussed whether to make changes to the website or to launch a new one. You may even have started on the design and content. We launched a new look for the hotel with a theme that now runs throughout our marketing. A professional looking website need not be expensive. It is essential, however, that the design is attractive to potential customers. Look at other hotel sites to get a feel for what is standard in the hotel industry. Take note of any site that appeals to you and, in particular, any site that you feel would make you more likely to book a room if you were deciding on a holiday or business destination.

It is more important initially to have an actual site up and running than the look and feel of it. You can work on the design over time. If the site includes your contact details customers will be able to make a booking.

It does take time to design and to write the content for a new website. New customers will not notice if you have changed the site completely as long as they can see what is in store for them and can make contact. You should start work as soon as you can if you do plan to make changes or re-launch.

Advertising your tariff

You should also consider whether to advertise your tariff on your website. This will depend on the type of hotel you own. Most hotels give details of prices and this, in our opinion, will determine in most cases whether someone makes a booking. If a potential customer visits your site, likes what they see and then decides it is too expensive or too cheap they will probably not make a booking. If they are comparing you to a similar hotel and the other hotel has a lower tariff they will decide to book your competitor. In most cases they will do this without making contact with you. On the other hand, if you do not display your tariff it may appear that you are exclusive and therefore expensive. They may decide that your hotel is beyond their budget and not bother to make a call or send an e-mail.

We do not include our tariff on our website. We prefer to speak or communicate directly to enquiries. This gives us the opportunity to use personality or sales skills to secure a booking. If the decision is between your hotel and a competitor and price is the key consideration, you then have the chance to win the customer over. If they have already made this decision online without any direct contact you do not have this chance.

At the end of the day it is a personal preference whether you decide to include your prices. We don't believe that we would win more business just by displaying our tariff. It does of course depend on your prices and what type of customer you normally attract.

A light touch

A lady from France called to enquire about our tariff as she had noticed that our website did not provide this detail. When I supplied her with our prices she asked if we could offer a discount if she booked five rooms. She was looking for a base in the UK that would be easy for her family to meet at and involve the minimum amount of travel for each family member.

After she had enquired about the discount I asked her if she was indeed from France. She replied that she was. I informed her that we did not offer discounts to French people and she would have to pay the full rate. She laughed and asked me the reason for this.

My reply was that it was a well-known fact that the two nations had never exactly seen eye to eye and as such discounts were off the menu!

In hindsight I guess that this was a very risky response, particularly in light of today's current 'politically correct' atmosphere. It was a calculated risk, but the conversation was friendly and it was clear the caller enjoyed the banter. It was also an unexpected response. Usually hotels respond in a very impersonal manner. This is often mistaken for what some hotels consider to be professionalism.

When you run a small hotel there is room for the personal touch – in fact there isn't room for anything else. People respond to this even if they have become conditioned to the usual monotone responses given in today's world.

Setting up e-mail

You must also be accessible by e-mail. It is a necessary evil but it is also an excellent business tool. Telephone bookings are confirmed by e-mail and they save on the use of paper. We disconnected our fax machine within a few weeks. Even though we registered with a company to put a stop to unsolicited fax messages they kept coming and we received at least ten a day. Now and again a customer asks if they can confirm a booking by fax. When we explain that we no longer have a fax and ask for an e-mail they nearly always agree without any protest. It is interesting that many hotel booking agents are still relying on fax machines. E-mail is so much more direct and efficient. Yes, e-mails do not always arrive, especially if your service provider has an over-zealous spam filter, but fax messages often go astray or are chewed up by an underperforming piece of hardware. E-mails do not require paper and can be stored without the need for additional physical space.

If the hotel already has an e-mail address you should keep this if you can. This may well involve staying with or joining the existing service provider. If you join or bring with you your own service provider you may well have to change the e-mail address. You may consider the existing address is not suitable. However, continuity is vital when you start out. As long as you have an e-mail address and guests can reach you, you can decide upon changes later on.

Initially we continued to use the previous owners' e-mail address as this had been detailed in advertising and was included in the hotel brochure. However, we did not wish to continue with this for too long as we preferred to use a different service provider and one that offered broadband. The existing internet service relied on a dial-up connection which was far too slow.

We now have two e-mail addresses. We use one for reservations (reservations@ hotelname.com) and one for general mail (hotelname@isp.co.uk).

Being available

You must ensure that potential customers can contact you at whatever time they choose. We receive telephone calls at 11 p.m. and sometimes in the middle of the night. We also take calls as early as 6.30 a.m. You will not need to change the hotel telephone number but you may wish to switch suppliers if this is possible and if it makes financial sense. This is something you can decide upon over the course of the first few months. All of the previous marketing collateral will include the hotel contact information and any change will have an impact on your customers.

Final thoughts

Your first few days will be tiring and stressful. They should also be enjoyable and you will begin to get a feel for whether the hotel trade is for you or not. Do make time to relax and do other things. This will be difficult at first but it is important to look after your own welfare. Go to bed early if you can and don't drink alcohol to excess. You will need all of your energy if you are to get through the first few days and weeks.

7
A year in the life of a hotel owner

Managing day to day – more of what nobody will tell you!

If you have always dreamt of working for yourself, owning and running a small hotel is the perfect way to start. If this is your first business venture you will enjoy the freedom of not having to answer to anyone. Many people choose to own a hotel for this reason alone. What you need to realise is that this also brings a great deal of responsibility. You have to make your own decisions every day – there is nobody else to turn to for the final say. This in itself is liberating. It is fun having to make your own decisions, even if you make the wrong choice. If you learn from each decision that you make and do not beat yourself up too badly when you mess up, you will enjoy this side of the job immensely.

Relying on your staff

Your staff will ask you how to do things, even if they have worked in the hotel for some time. When they do, it is an opportunity to explain how you would like to see things done. Your staff should also inform you if anything is in need of your attention. You might find this annoying to start with – we did. Having your cleaner or housekeeper continually reminding you that a lock needs fixing, a light bulb changing or a drain unblocking can be tedious.

> We encourage our staff to tell us about anything that is in need of repair or if they feel something should be executed in a different way. We do not have time to check every nook and cranny each day and we rely on our staff to help us keep the hotel in a good state of repair.

During the winter months, the hardest thing to do in your first year is to get out of bed in the morning. It will be dark and often cold or raining, or both. If you are not used to an early start it is even harder.

> A few weeks before our move we realised that our lives would change completely. I very rarely left my bed before 8 a.m. I decided that if the future held early mornings as my fate and I would have to be up at 5.54 a.m. every day, I would lie in until 8.30 a.m., at least until the day came when things had to change. This was a mistake. I should really have started to leave my bed at 5.54 a.m. in an effort to become accustomed to my new routine.

Early starts become much easier when you reach your second winter. Knowing that you have to be up at a certain time each day also helps. Your guests are relying on you and expect that all will be functioning normally when they come down to breakfast or to check out.

Using overseas staff

It was reported in the daily newspapers recently that hotels now prefer to employ staff that are not from the UK. The report said that overseas nationals are more willing to work and are more reliable, though it did not mention how many of the overseas staff already working in the UK hotel industry could actually speak English. However, it did mention that employing non-UK residents is likely to be short term and that overseas staff are more likely to leave when the desire to go home becomes too great.

With a small hotel, depending on your location, employing local people may be your only option. People who work in hotels usually do so for the convenience. They do not want to travel for over 45 minutes. Economically it is not viable for them to spend most of their wages on getting to and from work. Employing local people can also pay dividends as they will help you to spread the word and more people will know about your hotel. Overseas staff might well cost less and they will possibly be satisfied with the minimum wage. However, they will not necessarily know very many people in the local area or have a strong enough command of the English language to recommend you to others.

One of the most astonishing claims made in the report was that the head of one of the UK's largest industry bodies had been quoted as saying that cleaning rooms and waiting on tables is not difficult and therefore it doesn't really matter who you employ! While this might be true in the larger hotels where guests do not need to speak to the staff that often, in a small hotel your staff will come into contact with your guests every day. It is vital that they can converse politely and cheerfully. They may also be asked for information and locally based staff are more likely to be able to assist.

Cleaning staff

Cleaning rooms is hard work. If you clean a room effectively it takes time. Yes, it is a job that you do not need any qualifications for. But you do need to have the right attitude and take pride in what you do.

Waiting staff

Although waiting on tables is straightforward enough, you do need to have staff working for you that are cheerful, presentable and polite and have your guests' best interests in mind. You need staff that are on the ball and deliver what the customer has asked for without any complication. This is more difficult first thing in the morning – some people are not very good at early mornings. You need consistency. There is no point in having people work for you that are happy one minute and in a mood the next. There is more to waiting on tables than meets the eye. Your guests will notice if the waiter or waitress is grumpy. Breakfast and dinner times are two of the main reasons why guests rebook, and this is why it is crucial that you have staff working for you that present the most professional image at all times.

If you employ a cook and waiting staff for the breakfast period it is still your responsibility to ensure that guests are catered for and that breakfast starts and ends on time. This involves you opening the hotel up first thing. Even if you employ others to handle the kitchen, as owner the buck stops with you. Close supervision when you start out will give you time to judge whether the people you have working for you are performing to your required standards.

> When we first started we had two waitresses and a cook. We had no experience whatsoever of working in a commercial kitchen. The hotel has to be opened up every morning in time for when guests first appear from their rooms. We didn't feel that this was a task we should leave to the kitchen personnel. We feel that, as we are responsible for the premises, we should be available at this time. It is also important that you have close contact with your guests and that they know you are the owner. Whatever the size of the establishment, guests enjoy speaking to and being looked after personally by the owner.

If your cook or waiting staff are not available to work, you will have to take over their role. If you start out working in the kitchen from day one and learn the ropes by taking an active role, when the day comes that you have to cook the breakfast or wait on tables you will be ready.

> We parted company with our cook after six months. As I had worked in the kitchen from day one I felt reasonably comfortable, if somewhat nervous, at taking over the cooking. It is now my favourite time of the day and I draw a great deal of satisfaction from cooking breakfast for our guests.

Doing it all yourselves

With a small hotel you may not have sufficient budget to justify having a cook, waiter, cleaner, housekeeper and receptionist. If you are running the hotel together you will be in a position to fill these roles yourselves when this is necessary. If you decide not to have staff and your hotel is busy most of the time be wary of taking on too many of the daily chores. It is tempting to look at your budget and on paper decide that you would save money by employing no staff at all. This is a false economy.

To cook breakfast, wait on tables, clean all of your rooms, answer the telephone, reply to e-mails or faxes, man reception, deal with the post, go shopping, order supplies, answer the front door, service your guests, prepare for dinner and clean the kitchen and all of the general areas used by guests will take all of your time, every day of the week. If you manage all of these jobs yourselves you will have little or no time left in the day for other essential business activities such as marketing and accounting. You will also exhaust yourselves.

To clean ten rooms efficiently will take the two of you at least four hours. One person cleaning alone would take much longer and would not have the time available to clean each room thoroughly. This alone is the best motive for employing someone else to do the cleaning for you. A clean room is a basic requirement for anyone staying in a hotel and is another of the key reasons why people rebook.

Being the fount of all knowledge

Your guests and the people that book guests into your hotel have little understanding of what it takes to manage a business of this kind. Why should they? As a result they expect you to be available all of the time and to be on top form. They expect you to answer all of the questions they pose immediately. You are an information source to them. Fulfilling this role is not as difficult as it sounds. If you are new to the area and have no idea where the local bus or train station is or which is the best local restaurant or the best taxi firm, your preparation before you take over is key. When a guest asks you to recommend the best restaurant or public house or where the nearest cinema is located, you need to know.

If you employ local people they will be able to answer this for you. Ask them as soon as you arrive for details of the local amenities. You will then be more prepared for the questions your guests ask.

Doing it right

Over time you will be asked all sorts of questions. You will learn the answers and be better prepared if you keep a record of the information you give to customers at the time they make their enquiry. If you are unable to give them the information that they need, take the time to find out for them. It is simple enough. The internet is the first port of call and in most cases this offers an immediate solution. We are often asked how far we are from various nearby villages or places of interest. A simple search on www.theaa.com or on Google™ maps gives you the distance and directions to most places.

Doing it wrong

If you are unhelpful and say that you do not know, leaving it to the guests to find out for themselves, it gives the appearance that you do not care. If, on the other hand, you are seen to do as much as you can to find out for them, they will remember this next time they decide whether to stay with you. Don't expect to always receive the thanks that you feel your efforts deserve. Customers paying for their room and rebooking are sufficient praise.

What questions to expect

Some of the questions you will be asked at one time or another include the following:

- How far are you from the nearest train/bus station?
- Could you book me a taxi for 7.30 a.m.?
- Where is the nearest cinema?
- Could you recommend a good restaurant?
- Could I arrange for an early morning call at 5.30 a.m.?
- Where is the nearest public house?
- Does my room have cable TV?
- Does the hotel have broadband facilities?
- I have forgotten my toothbrush/shaver, where can I buy one?
- Can I leave my car in your car park during the daytime?
- How do I find your hotel?
- Do you cater for vegetarians?

- Can we have breakfast in bed?
- Can I borrow an adapter plug?
- Do you have facilities for the disabled?
- Do you take all major credit cards?
- Do you have an iron and ironing board I can use?
- Does you hotel have a lift?
- I have forgotten my mobile phone charger. Do you have one that I could borrow?
- Do you have a dry cleaning service?
- I need to do some washing. Do you have facilities for this?

Dealing with sales calls

You will receive numerous calls every day of the week from people trying to sell you something. Most will be cold calling and will not know the size of your organisation. They will assume that you are a potential customer and that you have the ability to spend hundreds if not thousands of pounds with them. If this becomes apparent at any time during the call you will know that they are not worth spending time on. Any company hoping to secure your business will behave professionally and will not expect you to commit over the telephone or on the strength of one sales visit. If they do, it is a safe bet that they are just trying to extract money from you and will not give you value in exchange.

> We were not prepared for the number of calls that we receive. Even though we had run a business before we were never exposed to the plethora of companies all vying for business in the hotel trade. If you have received several similar calls on the same day or week it is difficult to be polite to the person you are speaking with. These calls are time-consuming and quickly become annoying.

You can speak with your telephone supplier about blocking nuisance calls. The problem with this is that every now and then you get to speak to a really useful supplier. You may also speak, purely by chance, to a company offering something that you actually need right away. This doesn't happen that often, but it does occur from time to time. In addition to these calls you will receive the same number of e-mail sales messages. These are much easier to deal with as you can delete them in a second. It is advisable to briefly scan each e-mail for any useful data as the same applies to e-mails as sales calls. You might miss the offer that comes along every now and then that will be of use to you.

Over the course of a year you will hear from the same companies over and over again. This is acceptable. With small hotels you will not need to replace or buy certain items that often. For the suppliers it is a simple case of being in the right place at the right time. Keeping any useful contacts or data that come your way will make life easier for you when you do need to make a purchase.

Looking out for the scams and bogus offers

There are many companies out there trying to make you part with your money in exchange for little or no customer satisfaction and with the least possible effort on their part. There are also people trying to scam you and that will make offers to you that initially appear unbeatable or too good to miss. If the offer is too good to be true then in our experience it almost certainly is and should be avoided.

Watch out, scam about!

There are a couple of recurring calls from different sources to watch out for. One is a company that purports to achieve a listing for you on the first page of the various search engines on the internet. You are led to believe that when a potential customer searches for hotels in your region using specific key words they can guarantee that your hotel will be listed in the top ten on the first page. The service usually costs £199 or £299 per annum and they guarantee the service. You are asked for a prompt decision and they require payment in advance, by credit or debit card, before the service begins. The company usually has a website and will send you by e-mail confirmation of the details.

When such a company first contacted us it was a tempting offer. As a small business we have a limited budget for marketing. A position on one of the main search engines' first page is something every business aspires to. It can be achieved, but not by paying someone you have never worked with or ever heard of before to do it for you. The company that contacted us stated that they worked directly for the search engine owners and were the only company authorised to do so. While there are reputable search engine optimisation providers their fees are much higher. The main thing to remember is that if they want your money upfront after the first or second call, politely refuse their offer.

The other type of call we received nearly every week when we first started came from a call centre outside of the UK. They claimed to be the number two telecommunications provider in the country and as such could save us substantial amounts on the cost of our telephone calls. We are always interested to speak with people who say they can save our business money. When we first spoke to this particular company the caller spoke for several minutes without a pause. He was obviously based overseas. Interrupting his flow made no difference he just continued to rant. He then made a mistake by asking if the business ran a switchboard which required the caller to dial '9' to get an outside line. When the reply was affirmative he said that his company could not help our type of business and he hung up.

Each time we received a similar call the only aspect of the caller's sales patter that had changed was the name of his company. Initially it was easy to have fun when taking a call of this nature. If the caller was prepared to waste our time he must be game for having the same thing done to him in return. Thankfully we do not receive this type of call anymore.

There are similar scams that arrive by e-mail. One such e-mail really is a nuisance. It is hard to believe that anyone would fall for such nonsense. The enquiry is usually to book a room or rooms for two or three weeks for a date two or three months ahead. The e-mail asks for full details of your tariff and availability. If you have not received this type of enquiry before they are not easy to spot. If you regularly attract overseas guests they are even harder to detect. We replied to the first e-mail of this nature and were optimistic that we would receive a booking for a guaranteed period of several weeks. The reply to our message arrived a week or so later. It confirmed the booking and asked how we would like to receive payment: payment that would be sent in full in advance of the stay. This is when alarm bells began to ring. People do not usually offer to pay in full several weeks in advance of their stay. Why on earth would they do this?

The next e-mail we received exposed the scam. The contact wanted to pay several thousand pounds more than the tariff, with the proviso that we would pay by credit card for the guest's additional travel costs. In this instance it included the guest's flights and a hire car. In another e-mail they wanted us to pay for the guest's training course.

One of the ways to spot this scam is from the name of the contact. It is usually an English name but one that is derived from an English word that is not necessarily a name. Our first contact was Dr David Cheese. Subsequent e-mails were from people with even more ridiculous names (my apologies to anyone genuinely with such a name). This signifies that the e-mail comes from overseas from people with a poor understanding of the English language. The e-mails often contain phrases in English that people in this country no longer use.

You may or may not already have heard about these types of communications. The lesson to be learned is not to give your business or personal bank or credit card details to anyone by e-mail or over the telephone unless you are 100% aware of their identity.

Erring on the side of caution

You can never be completely certain who you are dealing with over the telephone or by e-mail, but it is sound business practice to be polite to anyone you come into contact with. They could possibly be a future customer or will remember you when a colleague or friend asks them to recommend a hotel.

However, your time is precious. Minutes spent talking to someone you have no intention of doing business with is time you could spend promoting the hotel or having a break.

The hoax and time-wasting calls do diminish after a few months but it is easy to be caught off guard. To avoid this you should question and take time to consider any proposal offered to you. Any serious business will be prepared to wait for an answer.

Dealing with customer behaviour

You will be surprised at how people behave in your hotel. If you live in the hotel it is your home too. If you live in a house in the grounds it will still be part of your life. Having guests share your home takes some getting used to. If you live in a separate part of the hotel that is private, you will still find that guests wander unexpectedly into your living room or kitchen from time to time. This is going to happen and there is little you can do about it, other than to keep all of your doors locked. Even signs do not deter guests from being in places they shouldn't – people do not always notice signs.

Your guests will bring all of their habits, good and bad, into your environment. Some will be incredibly neat and tidy and you will not notice them. Other guests will treat the place literally 'like a hotel'. If they know that someone else cleans their room they will leave more of a mess. The tidy guests clear up after themselves and make the bed. The messy guests leave wet towels on the bedroom floor and scatter their belongings everywhere.

Some take all of the toiletries home with them, regardless of whether they have used them. The same guests eat as much as they can at breakfast and take fruit and yoghurt away with them. If you leave sweets in reception they may even empty the bowl. If they smoke they may smoke in their room in spite of it now being against the law.

Some guests do not use the bath or shower. Presumably they prefer the comfort of their own bathroom. Some guests will eat a takeaway meal in their room, even if this against hotel policy. They will bring their own alcohol rather than pay hotel prices.

You have to remember that when someone stays in a hotel they are paying for the privilege. They will expect to be looked after. If you do look after them, are cheerful, polite, happy and always prepared to take time to chat with them, it is more likely that they will respect your hotel and behave as if they were at home. One of the biggest compliments a guest can pay you is to tell you that they always feel at home when they stay with you. Guests that do so will return and will tell their friends, family and colleagues about you.

You will have to deal with awkward or impolite guests. You will have to deal with troublesome guests from time to time. You will have to admonish suppliers and staff that let you down. It is how you handle these situations that will determine the outcome of any incident.

Dealing with customers – customer service is everything!

If your business is to become a success, each guest that stays with you must be treated as a source of potential future business. You need each guest to want to return to your hotel whenever they visit your area, and you want them to recommend you to their colleagues, friends and family. This is the best form of advertising and it is free.

If you own a hotel in a holiday destination you need your guests to return each year, or more frequently. You need them to tell their friends and family about the wonderful hotel they holidayed in for two weeks, the warm hospitality they received, the outstanding food and the immaculate room they stayed in.

If you rely on business trade the same applies. Many business travellers return to the same area time after time. They have colleagues who do the same and have frequent contact with their own customers. They also have friends and family. Repeat business is a sign that you are providing the best possible environment for your guests.

A good way of deciding how to handle your guests is to think back to the times when you have stayed in a hotel. Consider how you were welcomed, what annoyed you, what pleased you and whether you would return to the same hotel. Contemplate how you expect to be treated when you stay somewhere. If you apply this to how you behave towards your guests you will have happy customers.

Coping with rudeness

We treat all our customers in the same way. We are always polite and friendly. We will make the best possible attempt to assist them whenever they call upon us to do so. If a customer is rude or discourteous you must learn not to take it personally. Never mirror their behaviour. If you find this difficult, try harder. Eventually it will become second nature to always be cheerful and helpful. We enjoy looking after our customers and it is one of the pleasures of the job. In return you will reap the benefits.

One of the ways we cope with an impolite guest is to be friendly and helpful. We are never impolite in return. If the guest is downright rude this is a different matter. You do not have to put up with people who insult you or who swear at you. This is not acceptable in any situation. There is a way to handle this to your advantage. This involves politely asking the guest to refrain from behaving in this way or you will have to ask them to leave. You do not have to do this in an aggressive way. Asking politely and with a smile on your face will usually suffice. In most cases the guest will apologise and will not have realised that they had acted in a discourteous manner.

If a guest does not want to make small talk they will check in without any fuss and want to reach the tranquillity of their room as quickly as possible. This will not be because you have upset them in anyway. They will either be tired from their journey or have something on their mind. They might be desperate to visit the toilet. Whatever it is, they are not likely to tell a complete stranger.

You will learn in time how to deal with all types of customers. You will recognise which customers are happy to talk to you and which are not. The rude or impolite people stand out and it is easy to let this irritate you. Do not let this type of guest see that you are upset by their behaviour. Treat them as you treat everyone else.

Keeping up appearances

You can think whatever you like about your guests as long as you keep it to yourself. This can be fun. If you are checking in someone who infuriates you and has been a bit rude, you can call them all the names you wish to in your head, while at the same time smiling and wishing them a pleasant evening or holiday. You will find that if you are constantly cheerful with even the most annoying of people, eventually they will change their attitude towards you. If they don't but they continue to stay with you each week, or year, they are obviously happy with your hotel. You can draw a great deal of satisfaction from this.

Being consistent

If your receptionist is responsible for checking people into your hotel you must be confident that they will present the correct image. They must handle guests in the same manner as you. Consistency in this is vital. You do not want to spend all of your time building relationships with your guests to have this ruined by a receptionist who is offhand and unhelpful. It only takes a couple of words out of place and you are at risk of losing business.

Satisfying their every need . . .

Making your guests' stay with you enjoyable and memorable will result in future business. If you have been even the slightest bit rude at any time they will not come back.

Occasionally we have a guest who calls upon us for something at an awkward time of the day. This has happened in the early hours of the morning and at lunchtime when we have been taking a break. However annoying you find this – and you will find this annoying at some stage – do not let your customer know that you are vexed. They are not aware that they are causing you annoyance. When people stay in a hotel they expect to be looked after. Letting them see that they have upset you is a failure on your part. They do not expect this and it will not leave a good impression on them.

Worse for wear – and at their age . . .

We had a couple stay with us who were attending a wedding. The wedding was taking place at a venue just a five-minute walk away. On the first evening the couple returned from the pub at 1 a.m. and rang the front door bell as they had mislaid their key. We were in bed. When I arrived at the front door to let them in, the male guest was leaning against the front door and was having difficulty standing upright. His lady wife had disappeared. The wedding that they were attending was due to take place the next day. We were also hosting a wedding later that day and we had to be up at 5 a.m. to begin the preparations. We were not happy to be woken by drunken guests. It took several minutes to locate the female guest who had gone in search of somewhere to sit down. I found her in our garden to the rear of the hotel.

The male guest told me how lucky we were to have closed our bar as he wanted to continue drinking. He had no consideration for our situation and there was absolutely no point in discussing this with him. As an event manager I had had plenty of experience dealing with drunken middle-aged people and one of the key lessons learned was never to argue with them about anything. As they were staying another night I made a note to remind them the next day to take their key out with them. I joked that if they locked themselves out again they could sleep on the bench in the garden. It was an effort to keep the conversation on a friendly level. I was determined not to show my annoyance and entered into light-hearted banter with them both.

They were concerned that they had also locked themselves out of their room. A quick visit to the room discovered that they had left the key in the door. They admitted that they quite often did this. Just to add insult to injury their room was on the third floor. I helped them up the stairs and made sure they made it to the room safely, not wishing them to disturb the other guests. I made it back to bed at 2 a.m.

These incidents are few and far between in a business hotel. The couple were staying over a weekend, it was a balmy evening and they had enjoyed themselves. The next day they apologised for the way they had behaved and we had no more trouble from them. They spent time with some friends at our bar the next afternoon and were appreciative of their surroundings. The thought in my head when I spoke to them helped me to get through the incident without letting them know how obnoxious they had been: 'I hope that when I reach 65 years of age I will have grown out of going out on the town and getting hopelessly drunk!'

Tantrums, chocolates and rose petals

A couple booked a double room with us for a Saturday in June and mentioned that they were attending a wedding reception in a local public house. They confirmed the booking by e-mail. We had three other couples staying with us that day and they were all guests at different weddings.

The day before they were due to stay with us the gentleman called to ask if he could leave his car in our car park on the Friday evening. The couple arrived to check in at 6 p.m. the next day. Meeting them for the first time revealed that they were in fact the happy couple and had been married that afternoon. They were checking in ahead of returning to the evening reception. The bride was experiencing difficulty standing up and had obviously enjoyed too much champagne. She sat at our bar while her new husband checked in. They disappeared to their room shortly after. Forty minutes later the bride reappeared. She was extremely upset and complained to our receptionist about the room that they had been allocated. Our receptionist called us and asked if we could come over to resolve the problem.

When we arrived the bride was shouting, almost screaming, and in tears. She complained bitterly that their room was not adequate and not what she had expected on her wedding day. She went on to say that the beam in the room was a major obstacle for her husband as he was so tall. She asked if we could remove it!! It transpired that she was more upset that the room was not decked in garlands and flowers and that no effort had been made on her special day. In her country of origin this was common practice and expected.

We mentioned that they had not informed us of their plans when they called to book the room. The husband looked very sheepish and admitted that he had forgotten to tell us. He thought that because he had said that they were at a wedding reception and had asked to park in our car park the night before, we would automatically assume that they were getting married.

Unbeknown to us at the time, the bride had knocked on other guests' doors and had asked them to pay a visit to their room to view how upsetting the situation was for her. One guest offered to swap rooms with them.

We offered to let them move to a different room. It was upsetting to be spoken to in this way by someone who should have been enjoying her big day. We discovered later that the bridegroom had been in charge of all of the arrangements and that all had not gone to plan throughout the day.

Even though we made the offer to switch rooms for them the bride continued with her tirade. She became personal in her attack and at this stage I decided that enough was enough. I explained that we would move them to a room with no beams and with high ceilings and that we would arrange to decorate the room, only if the bride calmed down. If not, they would be looking for somewhere else to stay. This instantly had the desired effect and the situation moved on to a much friendlier basis.

With wedding couples we always include flowers and chocolates in the room with a wedding card, and on most occasions a bottle of champagne. In this instance another wedding couple had recommended us to them and our guests were disappointed to find that we had not offered the same service that their friends had enjoyed.

By the time they had swapped rooms and departed to attend their reception it was 8 p.m. The bride had offered to pay cash to place flowers in the room and cover the bed in rose petals. I declined the money and agreed to her request anyway. She had become very tearful and upset by her own behaviour. She was more upset that her wedding day was not all she had hoped for.

Finding rose petals and flowers at 8 p.m. on a Saturday evening is something of a challenge. We had already given them a bottle of champagne which they had consumed before they left for the reception. Our neighbours run a party and catering business and they ensured that we fulfilled the wedding couple's demands. The room was bedecked with flowers and balloons and we left chocolates on the pillow. We covered the bed in rose petals.

The next morning the couple did not come down for breakfast. On checking out it was obvious that the bride was seriously hungover. She did thank us for the effort we had made with the room but at no stage did either of them apologise for the way in which they had behaved.

As a result of this incident we now ask anyone who books and mentions they are attending a wedding whether it is actually their big day. In most cases people tell you this anyway and make contact with you on numerous occasions to check the booking and confirm arrival time.

We did not expect an apology from the couple. They didn't cause any damage and the entire scene quickly took on a situation comedy, almost slapstick feel. At one stage when I was showing the bride the new room she burst into tears and flung her arms around me! I prayed that the bridegroom wouldn't walk in to find his new bride being comforted by a total stranger next to the marital bed!

This was a highly unusual scenario and demonstrates that anything can and does happen when you own a hotel. You must learn from such experiences. At no stage were we rude to the guests and we did not return their insults with rudeness. We tried to take the heat out of the situation as soon as we could. When we had done so we went out of our way to help them. We took great pleasure from meeting their demands and not letting them leave the hotel with a poor opinion of us.

While you have to see the funny side of this type of situation you must also take the guests seriously and not let them know what you are thinking.

Enforcing the no-smoking laws

Now that smoking in public premises is against the law it is much easier to deal with people who do continue to smoke in your hotel. By law you must make provisions for doing so. If you do not and the authorities discover that you have effectively allowed customers to smoke on your premises you will receive a hefty fine. We have found that since the smoking ban came into effect on 1 July 2007, most smokers respect the law. Before 1 July we already had a no-smoking policy; however, guests quite often ignored this and smoked in their room. It was more difficult to reprimand them as they were not breaking any law by doing so.

You can always tell when someone has smoked in his or her room. If you are absolutely certain that they have done so then you must take action. You must be careful though, as even when you think it is obvious that they have been smoking there could be another explanation. The best solution is to speak to the guest when they are alone or send them an e-mail. Simply explain to them that when you were cleaning the room you could smell smoke and that you found cigarette ash on the carpet or a cigarette end in the bin. Remind them that they must not, by law, smoke in the hotel, and that if they do you could receive a hefty fine.

Most guests will deny that they have smoked in the room even if they have done so. The point is that you will have let them know that you are onto them. If you have the same problem again with them, you must issue a stronger warning that failure to comply with the law will result in you not being in a position to accept a booking from them again.

Getting your facts right

You must be certain of your ground when confronting someone in this way and it is safer to approach the matter in a conciliatory way. We had some overseas guests stay with us for a few days. On the first day of their stay our cleaner found a cigarette end in a bin in one of their bathrooms. On checking the other guests' rooms she discovered more cigarette ends in bins.

We sent an e-mail to the person who booked the rooms and asked them politely to speak with the guests and advise them of the new law. Only one of the guests spoke English. When they returned to the hotel in the evening I spoke with the English-speaking guest and explained what the cleaner had found. She was smoking a cigarette outside of the front door to the hotel at the time. It transpired that she had smoked outside the hotel with the other guests in her party on several occasions. They had not wanted to leave litter in the street by discarding their finished cigarette. They had extinguished the cigarette and then placed it in the dustbin in their rooms. Our cleaner had noticed that the rooms in question did not smell of smoke although the evidence in the bin pointed to a crime being committed.

It was quite a shock to meet people who are so concerned for the environment that they would not litter the streets. I had to point out that even though the cigarette had been extinguished, placing it in the bin inside the hotel represented a fire hazard. The guest agreed to leave the litter on the pavement on the proviso that I cleaned up each time she did so.

The biggest lesson we have learned from all the dealings we have had with our customers is not to take anything personally. People come in all shapes and sizes, have good and bad traits and will not lose any sleep over you, though the majority of guests are considerate and friendly.

Catering for regular guests

If you have lots of regular customers you will get to know more about them as they will about you. Our weekday clientele are nearly all regulars and stay two or three nights a week. All guests are important to a small hotel and the more regulars you have the easier life becomes. You must ensure that you cater for them first and that you have availability for them if they are booking week on week. You will get to know their habits, what time they arrive and when they have breakfast. This helps you to plan your day and makes it easier to look after them.

Managing communications

The telephone and the internet are two of the most powerful tools for running any business. With a hotel they are your lifeblood. Your customers and potential customers must be able to contact you at any time. You must be prepared to respond to them quickly and demonstrate that you are always available to them.

Responding to enquiries

Responding promptly to enquiries is a must. If you do not, your potential customer may book a rival hotel and the business could be lost forever.

Your website must include your contact information. This must be clearly visible and easy to find. We have found that the majority of booking enquiries we receive are made by telephone. Any e-mail enquiry is answered as soon as it arrives or, if this is not possible, at the earliest convenient time.

We request that all bookings made by telephone are confirmed by e-mail. We discarded our fax in favour of e-mail after we found that the majority of people have access to the internet.

It is vital to demonstrate that your hotel is run professionally and communications play a key role in this. How you answer the telephone and reply to e-mails are normally the first indications of the type of business you run. First impressions are extremely important when a booking is at stake.

Answering the telephone

When you answer the telephone you must always be polite, have a clear voice and be welcoming. Your tone when you answer must be professional. We always answer in the same way by saying good morning/afternoon/evening followed by the name of the hotel.

Answering e-mail

When answering e-mail communication the principle is the same. We always address the sender as Mr or Mrs/Ms and we thank them for their enquiry before confirming availability and the tariff. Small hotels do need to behave professionally and it is essential to deal with all enquiries as soon as they are received. If you don't you risk losing a booking and if the caller books elsewhere you may also be losing valuable future business.

Providing a professional response

People contacting you will not always be aware of the size of your business. They expect a friendly welcome from a professional receptionist. Many ask to be put through to the reservations department. We never correct them and simply reply by saying 'reservations speaking'.

We take full details of any booking received by telephone and request confirmation in writing via e-mail. We ask for the name of the guest or guests, the name of the caller, their telephone number and if they are not a regular customer we ask for credit or debit card details to guarantee the room. All of these details are important. If the guest later cancels the room or for any reason fails to materialise you have proof of the booking and can charge a cancellation fee.

Choosing your telecoms provider

Choosing a telecommunications provider will largely depend on your location. Some areas have just one or two options to choose from. A switchboard with ISDN lines coming into the hotel allows you to accept calls from multiple callers. It also allows customers to dial out even if you or other guests are on a call.

While this is useful, we find that guests vary rarely use the telephone in their room to make or receive a call. Our hotel has four ISDN lines. This, in theory, means that we can be on the line with a call holding and two guests can make a call at the same time. This will never happen. Most people now own a mobile phone and are happy to use this in preference to the telephone in their room. This has made the hotel bedroom telephone effectively redundant.

Call charges

Hotels have historically charged a small fortune for using the telephone. This has alienated hotel guests to the point that they would sooner walk to a phone box than pay through the nose for a two-minute call. Our switchboard has software that logs all calls and we can produce an invoice from this. The previous owners chose to add 50% to the cost of each call in an effort to increase revenue. In 18 months we have been in a position to charge just two customers for lengthy telephone calls. Both were overseas calls and their mobile telephones did not work in this country. As such we have made a grand total of £2.75 from our state-of-the-art telephone system!

We could have made a bit more but we couldn't bring ourselves to charge a handful of customers seven pence for a 30-second call. It just didn't seem right and we chose to foot the bill ourselves.

We took over our telephone system and signed a two-year contract with the supplier before we arrived. It was the only way to ensure continuity. The hotel does not need four lines of ISDN yet we are tied into the contract with penalty fees if we cancel. At no stage did the supplier explain their service – they simply assumed we knew what we needed. In turn we chose the same options as the previous owners. We did not have time to investigate the telephone system until two months into our ownership. We had more pressing issues to deal with.

When we did call in the telecommunications provider to discuss our business needs we explained that the guests did not use the telephones and that we needed to explore other options. The local business manager who came to see us attempted to sell us a hopelessly expensive and completely ineffective alternative solution. The idea was for us to buy new hardware that would allow customers to make cheaper telephone calls than they could make with a mobile phone. The system would cost several thousand pounds to install and all that we had to do would be to encourage our guests to use the telephone in their room. We would achieve this apparently by advertising the lower call charges to guests as a viable alternative to their mobiles.

This demonstrated the total lack of understanding of our needs and of the trends within the hotel industry. Having a telephone in a guest bedroom is an outdated service, many of the industry bodies controlling the hotel rating system having in the past included the bedroom telephone as an essential service to customers and one that enhances a hotel's grading.

This is now absurd. The only use for a telephone in a guest bedroom is in case of an emergency and for contacting the owner or another room. However, in a small hotel guests use their mobile phones to contact another room 99.9% of the time and in most cases go to reception to speak to the owner.

Keeping up with technology

There are now a number of suppliers working with small hotels on installing broadband into each room at a cost-effective rate. This service is still in its infancy. Telecommunications companies and telephone providers seem obsessed with making as much money as possible out of their customers before they realise there are alternatives.

Our building is over 300 years old. Hard wiring telephones and the internet to each bedroom is expensive. Wireless technology in a building with four-foot thick walls is still proving to be a major obstacle and is unproven as a suitable solution. It is also expensive.

All hotels wish to keep pace with the ever-changing technology available today. It would be the perfect scenario to have broadband internet access and cable or satellite TV in every room. If your hotel already has these services installed and the cost is competitive you have an advantage that will prove to be a draw to all guests and potential customers.

If you do not have these services and wish to have them installed you must find the most cost-effective and reliable solution from a supplier that understands your business. You must weigh up whether your guests would really benefit and if the cost of installation and the monthly contract fee is worth the outlay.

Some suppliers will entice you with offers which allow you to justify the cost based on passing this on to your customers. This involves charging them for access to the internet or to films or other TV services. You have to ask yourselves whether you would be willing to pay for these if you were the guest. While many of these services are available to guests staying with one of the major hotel chains they do not transfer easily to the small hotel sector and very few suppliers or providers have adapted to meet the demands of the small business. Although these companies do cater for smaller hotels the cost is usually prohibitive.

Choosing the services you will provide

The services that you offer to your guests in their rooms also depends on the type of hotel you run. Do people on a two-week holiday sit in each night and watch a film on cable TV? They may do once or twice during their stay or if they have small children. You need to decide if this is something you can afford to do and if it will increase trade. Bear in mind that guests will be willing to watch a film or sporting event on a cable or satellite channel in the guests' lounge. It may also be more cost-effective to include a DVD recorder in each room and have a DVD library available.

Do businessmen really need to use the internet when they have been working all day? When we first started we thought that they would. It is the sort of thing, we thought, that businessmen do when they are away from home and have nothing else to do other than work. During the time we have been here only a handful of guests have asked if we have internet access. When we purchased the hotel it had dial-up access available in each room. With the introduction of broadband this method of access is now largely defunct. If a guest is in urgent need of the internet we allow them to use the broadband installed in the office.

When businesses catch up with the technology that is already available, most people will be able to access the internet via their mobile phone. You may also provide broadband in the hotel reception or lounge or wirelessly within these rooms and the dining area. As a small hotel you will, in time, be able to decide whether your guests really do need this type of service.

To install broadband and cable TV in every room is still expensive and unless you have a big budget and feel this is absolutely necessary you need to ask yourself whether the spend on this will bring in additional revenue to cover the cost.

Keeping track of bookings

As a ten-bedroom hotel we find it reasonably easy to keep track of the bookings we receive and of the customers that stay with us. We regularly receive calls from suppliers offering 'front of house' systems. Some have included the provision of a TV system in each room linked to the internet and displaying hotel information and advertising. Again this is the kind of service operated by much larger hotels as a matter of course. However, the product does not justify the expense, unless of course you have deep pockets. In an ideal world you would of course install every type of system offered to you to ensure that your guests' every whim is catered for.

We keep a handwritten diary of all bookings. Every booking is entered in pencil. The diary goes everywhere with us and is never out of our sight. We also keep a computer record of all bookings with payment details; these are entered at a later stage on a daily basis. We rely solely on the handwritten diary. As the entries are in pencil, if we have a cancellation this is easily erased and a new entry can be made.

The alternative is to use a computer, or even a network of computers with a PC or Mac in your office and one at reception. With a small hotel this is not something of that much benefit. It takes longer to use a computer to log a booking or to check someone in than to use a diary. If you make a mistake on a computer and accidentally delete a booking made by telephone you have lost it forever. Not so with a diary, unless of course you lose the entire thing. You can easily carry your diary with you depending on your schedule and you can rely on your receptionist to use it effectively with very little training.

Keeping it in perspective

Guests do not expect a small hotel to offer every latest advancement in technology. Generally they understand the economics of the situation. From the conversations we have with guests they prefer the comfortable homely feel of a small hotel to the more sterile environment of a large hotel. They also prefer the personal touch.

Hardware suppliers trying to sell or to rent the latest television technology often approach us. At the moment this is plasma or LCD technology. There are many similar companies all trying to cash in on the hotel market. Very few even make the effort to find out about your business before they make contact. The latest offer we received came from a door-to-door salesman hoping to tempt us with plasma TVs for £2.99 per week per room. The salesman didn't have technical data or even a picture of the merchandise. His opening pitch was to inform us that £2.99 was yesterday's price and that this had been reduced to £1.99. We suggested he come back in two days time!

Managing your bank account – not learning the hard way!

Depending on who you bank with, contacting your bank is in most cases a painful exercise. Gone are the days of speaking to your bank manager or speaking to your branch. You will almost certainly have to call an 08 prefix telephone number and when you do, speaking to an actual person can take a while. Contact and call centres are now the preferred option for banks when they decide how best to handle customer enquiries. As a business account holder, unless you are in the £1m plus turnover category, you are managed in pretty much the same way as a personal account holder. You will no doubt be allocated a business manager and will be 'guaranteed' a return call if you try to contact them. There is no guarantee, however, that your 'business manager' will know anything about your business or your industry.

Ensuring your bank account runs smoothly

As such, the onus is very much on you as a business owner to ensure that your account is managed effectively. In the hotel trade this is not as easy as it sounds. Your cash flow is dependent on your occupancy levels. If you rely on passing trade, or if you are not a tourist hotel or most of your bookings are made just a few days in advance, then managing your finances is made even more challenging.

Internet banking is essential; however, it is also unforgiving. Internet banking is not a system that accounts for cheque clearance; the majority of payments are made at the time of the transaction. If you make a payment online most banks will not make a charge for this. If you pay by cheque, direct debit, standing order or draw cash out many banks will charge you for the pleasure. The days of sending a supplier a cheque in the knowledge that it will take a couple of days to reach them and a further three or fours days to clear your account are fast disappearing.

If you make a payment online you are given the opportunity to choose when the payment is debited from your account. If you select the same day option the money leaves your account immediately. If you draw out cash at an ATM, by the time you arrive home and check your balance this latest transaction has already been debited to your account. Why then does it take up to ten days for your account to be credited if the customer has made their payment to you by debit or credit card when they checked out? Most card transactions take three or four days to be credited to your account. Until the banks decide to discontinue this so called service, you must manage your cash flow accordingly.

> We are led to believe by our card machine service provider that there are moves afoot to credit recipients' accounts with customer card payments the day after payment is made. Until such time you must manage your cash flow to take into account current banking practices.

This system may not be a surprise to you if you have owned or run a business previously, but the effect of having to wait for your money when you are relying on income to meet daily, weekly and monthly commitments is of greater concern when you run your own hotel. Each week you have to order supplies and pay for the numerous services that you receive, just to keep the hotel ticking over.

As with any business if you fail to make some payments on time you will find services withdrawn without much of a warning. This can be critical or even terminal as your guests rely on you for every service you have promised to them at the time they made their booking.

All is not lost, however. Internet banking is invaluable. It allows you to monitor your finances securely whenever you choose. Keeping daily tabs on your income and outgoings has never been easier. Making regular payments is routine. It is impossible to go overdrawn without prior authorisation; the system simply refuses the payment and often this does not attract the same bank charges that would be applied for a bounced cheque. It is not possible to pay someone unless the funds are available. This can be annoying, as you may have been waiting for several days for payments received to reach your account. There is no way of finding out when payments received will clear, they just appear either three, four or if a weekend intervenes five days after you are paid. Inexplicably they sometimes arrive after just two days.

Do not expect very much help from your bank if you find yourselves in financial difficulty. When there is a credit crunch many banks will not allow you to increase your overdraft, even if you promise to pay them back within a week or two and even if it is a life-or-death situation. This of course depends on which bank you have an account with. Some of the banks are much more aware of the type of business you run and as such are more likely to assist you through a difficult period.

All of this demonstrates why managing your finances has to be taken seriously. You have to maintain your bank account and keep it in order at all times.

> We review our account every day and we produce management accounts each month. We know exactly where we are, all of the time. This reduces the chances of being financially embarrassed. It ensures that our regular suppliers and essential services are paid on time, every time.

Planning when you pay the bills

There is no magic formula. All you can do to minimise worry is to plan when you make payments each month based on when you are most likely to receive income. This is one of the hardest aspects of running a hotel. There are certain services that have to be paid for, such as heating and lighting, your mortgage, insurance and so on. There are bills that you pay every week for food supplies and staff wages. You must keep a close eye on your account. When times are hard and occupancy levels are not what you had hoped for this is even more crucial.

Do not ignore bills and hope they will look after themselves. When they are received, plan when you will pay them and review this before you do to ensure it is necessary to make payment on that day.

Once you have run the business for 18 months or so you will know when you are most likely to be the busiest. Some lenders offer a seasonal repayment option allowing you to make increased mortgage payments over the most successful months and a reduced sum in the quieter period. The key to this, if you have this arrangement, is to remember that one way or another you will have to pay the mortgage in full. You must make provision for this in your financial plans.

> We pay our major suppliers once a month. Heating and lighting, rates and water, insurance and motor expenses are all timed for when we know we will have funds available to pay the direct debits we have set up. Wages are paid online every Wednesday and reach the staff's accounts by the Friday. Weekly supplies including food shopping and our egg delivery are paid at the time of purchase. All other weekly/monthly suppliers are paid in the first week of each month after our mortgage payment has been made. This structure for payments has proved to be successful but it has taken time to develop and is based pretty much on trial and error.

Using business debit and credit cards

Some banks will offer a business debit card. This allows you to make payments over an agreed period with the bank collecting what you owe them by direct debit once a month. It is also possible to have a business credit card. This works in the same way as a normal credit card and will attract interest charges. Both services, if used correctly, can offer you breathing space on paying for supplies or for unexpected costs.

Dealing with VAT

The other major outgoing is VAT. If you are VAT registered there are numerous options on when and how you make payment. HM Revenue and Customs will advise you on this. The one certain thing is that you do have to pay. We are on a flat rate scheme and paid 8.5% of turnover in the first year and 9.5% in the second. We settle the VAT every quarter. You must decide which method of payment works best for you.

One option is to open a separate account with your bank and save the VAT portion of all payments received. This ensures that you have sufficient funds available when your VAT bill arrives. However, in reality, during your first couple of years it will be difficult to save in this way.

When the time comes the VAT can be paid online. If you do decide to pay by this method you must arrange for the funds to leave your account four or five working days before the payment reaches the Revenue and Customs. You must also ensure that you quote your VAT registration number as the payment reference. If you do not your payment may well sit in a holding account pending investigation, and you will possibly receive a late payment notice from HM Revenue and Customs even though you have paid them on time.

Despite all this, we have found the VAT office easy to communicate with and very helpful when you do need to make contact with them.

Looking after yourself and your family

We chose to buy a small hotel for various reasons. Before we arrived we had no idea whether any of our plans would come to fruition.

When we were viewing hotels we met hoteliers that told us that they took at least one weekend a month as holiday and had two or three one- or two-week breaks a year. We know hoteliers that actually do this. They are not dependent to any great extent on income from the hotel and run the business more as a hobby. Lucky them!

Before we arrived we had hoped, naively, that we might at least be able to take a holiday once a year. Our initial plans included increasing occupancy levels at weekends and building and maintaining the regular custom. We took several weekends off over the first few months as hotel ownership did come as quite a shock to us once we started and we felt that we deserved a break. Equally the weekend occupancy level had not been that good and the previous owners had struggled to attract weekend trade. The hotel had only been open for three years when we took over and it does take time to establish a new hotel.

Considering your options

There are options open to any hotelier when they decide to take a holiday. They can close the hotel altogether. They can hire a temporary relief manager. They can leave the hotel in the hands of a close friend or family.

Closing the hotel

The decision to close the hotel altogether can depend on the type of hotel you own. You may have quiet periods during the out-of-season winter months when you have no custom whatsoever. Closing during such a period is much less of a risk than during a busy time of year. If you do take a holiday at this time you still need to be contactable or monitor communications from customers. You also need to consider what happens to the hotel when it is empty and unattended. This is when you need to have a close friend or family member or a trusted member of staff willing to keep an eye on things while you are away.

Hiring a relief manager

Hiring a relief manager is possible and there are agencies that specialise in temporary hotel personnel. You will need to spend a few days with the relief manager before you depart, showing them the ropes. You will also have to pay the agency a fee as well as the wages for the relief. You must also consider if you feel it is appropriate to leave your hotel in the hands of a total stranger.

We know hoteliers that hire a relief manager from an agency and are very happy to do so. We also know of hoteliers that leave their hotel in the hands of friends and family or have an agreement with another hotelier to cover for them in a reciprocal arrangement. This is not something we could ever imagine doing but everyone has a different outlook on running a hotel.

Finding someone you can trust

If you can find someone you trust to run the hotel for you while you take a holiday you will reap the benefits of having a relaxing break away from the stresses and strains of running your own business. At some stage you must take time out for yourselves.

We agreed to work as hard as we could for at least the first two years to ensure we learned as much about running the business as possible and to build on the previous owners' success.

We take holidays by arranging the occasional long weekend. These coincide with our quietest times and we never travel further than two hours away. We monitor our voicemail twice a day and return all calls if they are related to bookings or are of an urgent nature.

Keeping fit

Running a hotel does require a certain level of fitness. The day-to-day routine involved will help you to achieve this. If your hotel is busy most of the time there will be numerous different jobs that will need your attention every day. These will keep you active.

Just this morning I borrowed a ladder from a neighbour and cleared the hotel guttering of all the autumn leaves. This involved carrying a heavy ladder and climbing 20 feet to reach the gutters. Luckily, this only needs doing once a year! The alternative is to find a local tradesman to do it – which of course incurs a cost and takes longer.

We are mindful of our health. It is vital if you run the business together that you can cover for each other when one of you is unwell. Becoming ill is not something that you have time for. If an illness does strike you need to be reasonably fit to fight it off quickly. If you have something contagious you should not work in the kitchen or prepare food. This includes flu, colds and stomach disorders. Looking after yourselves takes on a new dimension and is not something we had considered that seriously before our livelihoods depended on it.

Spending time with the family

If you have a young family it is important to spend time with them. The joy of running our hotel is that we have a period during the day when we very rarely have guests on the premises. Between 10 a.m. and 4.30 p.m. our time is pretty much our own. We always find a couple of hours during this period to relax and unwind and spend time with our children. If we were working in an office somewhere this simply would not happen.

Unwinding

You must learn to find time during the day to rest and to do something that takes your mind off the hotel. Owning a hotel does require a great deal of energy and you can only replenish your energy levels by making time to rest and to exercise. If you meet your guests each morning in a state of permanent tiredness or with a hangover they will not be sympathetic. You are responsible for looking after them, not enjoying yourselves.

Having friends or family to visit you is a good way of unwinding. As long as they do not expect you to treat them as you would a guest and cook them dinner and be up early to prepare breakfast. Relaxing with friends and sharing your experiences with them is therapeutic. As long as you do not become boring!

In short . . .

However you decide to run your new business, make time for yourselves. It sounds simple on paper but is much more difficult in reality. If you want to make a success of your hotel you will need to find a balance between work and play.

How life changes – by people who know!

Every day is a new challenge when you own a hotel. The weight of responsibility can be a burden if you let it. It takes time to get to know your hotel. It takes time to settle into a totally new way of life. You must be patient and determined. A good friend once said that running a business is all about holding your nerve and sticking with it through thick and thin. Each time our backs are to the wall we remember these words.

There will be days when you question the sanity of your decision to uproot and take on a totally new life. Our feeling is based on the old saying 'nothing ventured, nothing gained'.

You will meet new people every day. You must welcome them and make them feel at ease if they are to become regular customers and recommend your hotel to others.

There will be days when you wake to the sound of your alarm and really wish you could stay in bed. As you are responsible for however many guests you have at the time, this is not an option. You have to get up every day, day in and day out.

If your hotel is busy during the holiday season or if you are busy all year round you will have periods when all you do for weeks on end is work. However, it was your decision to buy a hotel and you have to tough it out.

We have a lie-in on average once every other week. This is all year round. When we first started our new routine it was a complete shock to the system. Our breakfast times at the weekend are one hour later on Saturday and Sunday than on weekdays. We get out of bed an hour later and as such 6.54 a.m. instead of 5.54 a.m. is a lie-in. You do get used to this, usually when you are halfway through your second winter.

You will not be able to make a snap decision to spend a weekend away or visit a sick relative. You have to plan this well in advance to tie in with your occupancy or when you can arrange cover.

If employing people to work for you is a new experience, you will learn how to manage this in time, and it can be very rewarding. It is not simply a case of telling your staff what to do each day and expecting them to finish the job on time and to your standards. It is a case of working with them, encouraging them, looking after their needs, paying them on time, listening to them and being supportive if they need you to be. It is a challenge to offer your staff a stimulating environment in which to work. You need them to perform to a high standard each day. To do this you must involve them in the day-to-day management of the hotel and be friendly with them and get to know their background. We encourage our people to tell us if something needs changing or if they would do a task differently to make it easier.

The long and short of it

The message is simple. Running a hotel is a full-time occupation and requires dedication and your full attention at all times. It is a tie and a big responsibility and the only way to manage this is to take it seriously and to work harder than you have ever done before.

When we decided to buy a hotel I was working up to 16 hours a day seven days a week for several months at a time. I had a largely office-based occupation and sat for hours in front of a computer. I couldn't face another 15 to 20 years doing the same thing. I thought that running a hotel would be an easier life.

In some respects it is an easier life. We do not work 16 hours a day and we are not required to work every hour of every day. But we are permanently on call and responsible for our guests' and our staff's welfare at all times. We can't just up and walk out whenever we find it too difficult to cope.

There are aspects of your new life that you will enjoy immensely and areas that you find taxing. You will be out of your usual comfort zone at some stage each day and will have to make decisions for yourselves. This is fun if you have the right attitude. Solving a problem is satisfying as it has a positive effect on you and your business. You will have no boss to answer to or to tell you what to do. This is one of the best parts of the job and one of the reasons we chose this life.

Watching your business grow as a result of your efforts is the ultimate experience. This is not all about the profit that you make but the knowledge that your guests appreciate the service that you provide and rebook with you time and again.

Odd things can happen at any moment!

The beauty of owning and running your own business is that you are in control and you do not have to answer to a demanding boss – or to anyone for that matter. Running a business that is available to paying guests at any time exposes you to situations that you will not have come across before. That is part of the attraction, something different and unexpected happening at any moment.

An odd thing happened . . .

This morning after breakfast had finished and the guests had departed I sat down to write a section of this book. My family were away for the day so I had the chance of some peace and quiet. In time you will experience for yourselves that these types of moments are rare and that they are often interrupted.

Ten minutes had passed when I heard a car pull up in the customer car park. A distinguished, well-dressed looking gentleman alighted from a top-of-the-range perform-ance car and walked across the gravel towards the back door of the hotel. I went to greet him. Usually the back door is locked during the day and I did not want him to have to walk round to the front. I was intrigued, as we were not expecting any guests until later in the day. On Sundays guests tend to arrive late evening.

The gentleman, of about 65 to 70 years of age, had 'stopped by' to enquire whether the hotel was for sale. He had a relative interested in returning to the UK from overseas and he wanted to buy a business for them. He felt that a hotel would be an easy business to run and one that would not require any previous knowledge of the industry. He left his contact details and asked me to call him once I had considered his offer.

From his manner, the way he was dressed and the car parked on the drive it was clear he had been a successful businessman and that his intentions were serious. He was in a hurry and didn't really want to discuss very much. From the little I did discover about him it was clear that he would have the wherewithal to buy this type of business. Everyone has their price and it was all I could do to stop myself asking him how much he felt the business would be worth.

I had often daydreamed about a wealthy businessman appearing from nowhere and making a silly offer that we could not refuse. Today, we did not receive an offer as such, more of an enquiry, but this type of thing can happen at any moment.

After he had left I began to wonder if he was a crank or delusional. I also started to think about what he had said about the hotel industry and how easy it would be to run a hotel compared to other businesses. His relative had no experience whatsoever as far as I could ascertain. To him it would be the perfect business. Then I thought back to how I responded to my friends when I first told them I wanted to buy a hotel. 'It's easy,' I said. 'All you have to do is check people in, feed them breakfast and make their beds.'

I now feel annoyed with his comments yet I can fully understand the sentiment. It is a relatively attractive business as it does not require any previous knowledge or qualifications. It is, however, more involved than this and does require certain skills that not everybody has the privilege to possess. It does require patience and determination and an ability to adapt.

8
Diary of a hotelier

When we first decided to buy a hotel we had no experience of hotel management whatsoever. A visit to a high street bookstore resulted in the purchase of a couple of tomes which reportedly described what was required to buy and run a hotel. These were helpful up to a point. They detailed everything from the legal requirements through to designing a menu. What we were really looking for was someone to tell us what would happen to us each day, what to expect, a 'fly-on-the-wall' documentary-style description of what was in store for us. Unfortunately the books stopped short of going this far and we were a little disappointed. One of the things we realised is that the hotel industry is full of owners with different backgrounds and experience all with a unique way of running their hotel.

This chapter of the book is that 'fly-on-the-wall' account of what life is like for us. We have left nothing out – this is truly what happens each day. It is hoped that this will give you an insight into the everyday life of a hotel owner and prepare you for your own adventure.

Daily time schedule

5.54 a.m.	Alarm sounds
6.01 a.m.	Shower and dress (even at this early hour it is important to look presentable)
6.23 a.m.	Leave for hotel
6.25 a.m.	Arrive at hotel
6.25–7 a.m.	Open hotel and prepare for breakfast
6.45 a.m.	Waitress arrives (7.45 a.m. at weekends)

7.00–8.30 a.m.	Weekdays – cook breakfast for up to 12 guests each day
8.00–9.30 a.m.	Saturday/Sunday – cook breakfast for up to 20 guests each day
8.30–10 a.m.	Clean up after breakfast – kitchen and breakfast room
9.00 a.m.	Cleaners arrive
9.10 a.m.	Meeting to brief cleaners
10.00–10.15 a.m.	Prepare for breakfast the next day
10.15 a.m.–1.00 p.m.	Morning routine
1.00–2.30 p.m.	Lunch
2.30–7.00 p.m.	Afternoon routine
4.30–8 p.m.	Guests arrive to check in
7.00 p.m.	Monday to Thursday – evening receptionist arrives
11.00 p.m.	Hotel locked down for the night

The schedule

6.25–7.00 a.m.   Open hotel and prepare for breakfast

Each morning I arrive at the hotel and begin to prepare for breakfast. As I do all of the cooking the next person to arrive is our waitress at 6.45 a.m. She assists in setting up the breakfast room in preparation for the guests. On weekdays breakfast begins at 7.00 a.m. and ends at 8.30 a.m. At weekends we enjoy the luxury of a lie in with breakfast from 8.00 a.m. to 9.30 a.m.

We have contemplated starting 15 minutes later on weekdays as an experiment to see if this would be popular as most of our guests are business people visiting local companies. Then we realised that the only reason we had discussed this was because I would prefer an extra 15 minutes in bed in the morning. This is not a good enough reason to make such a change. We then looked at the closest competition and decided that our early start would work in our favour. Many business guests take breakfast at 7.00 a.m. as they opt to start work earlier. This gives them an opportunity to finish earlier or to have more time in the office without interruption.

We did explore the possibility of taking on a full-time cook or chef when we parted company with ours. Finding somebody to work at 6.30 a.m. and finish at 9.30 a.m. and who is reliable is not that easy. This will depend on where you are situated and how much of a journey your staff have to undertake.

The breakfast we prepare each day includes continental and full English. On the odd occasion we receive requests for something different and we do attempt to cover every eventuality. The majority of guests staying on a weekday chose a light breakfast or a combination of the full English ingredients. At weekends over 90% of guests opt for the full cooked breakfast with very few variations.

Over time we have made small changes to what we offer each day. The previous owners had already sourced good quality fare from a number of local suppliers. There is no point in fixing something that isn't broken. You must sample the food that you give to your guests on a regular basis. I recommend that any new waiting staff that we employ try each ingredient. I often taste the food. This ensures that you are maintaining the quality. Even if you are buying produce from the same source each time, the quality can vary and you need to ensure that this does not affect your business. By asking the staff to sample the food you ensure that they are confident that the food they deliver is satisfactory and of a high standard.

Some ingredients must be of a high standard whatever your budget. Other components of the perfect breakfast are of a similar standard wherever you purchase them. Breakfast is one of the key times of the day and your guests will consider whether to book with you again or try out a competitor based on how they feel about your breakfast.

Our full English includes two fried eggs, bacon, a sausage, fried tomato, fried bread and mushrooms. Scrambled or poached eggs can be substituted for fried and we only add beans if a customer requests them. If we have over 16 guests staying we provide just one fried egg but include beans. We have found that cooking two fried eggs per person takes much longer than just the one and beans only take a few moments to heat up.

When I first started in the kitchen working with our cook, the routine did not deviate from the set full English and when 20 guests stayed breakfast time was pandemonium. Cooking two fried eggs per guests delayed serving time to an unacceptable level.

Over time you will develop your own way of doing things. We have come up with a routine which suits our capabilities and that ensures our customers receive a good quality breakfast within an acceptable time frame. Practice, as they say, makes perfect.

Our bacon comes from a local farm. It is exceptional quality and guests remark upon the bacon more than any other ingredient. We order the bacon in four 5lb packs. This lasts about ten days during our quieter periods, and seven when we are busy.

A local farmer supplies our eggs and again these are delivered. The other ingredients we purchase from our local supermarket.

Our continental alternative consists of croissants, melon with seasonal fruit, yoghurts, prunes, cereal and fresh fruit. We buy the croissants part baked and frozen and these take 10–15 minutes in the oven to cook. The melon and fruit are sourced either from the main supermarket or our local grocer depending on availability and the season. We offer three different cereals, which guests serve themselves, and we also have packet cereals available to give a wider choice. We have experimented with other options, Danish pastries for instance; however, we ended up eating these ourselves.

When we first arrived it would take 30 minutes to set up for breakfast with two and sometimes three staff on duty. Mornings now involve just myself as cook and one waitress. I do most of the set up before the waitress arrives and it takes just 20 minutes. This is partly because I have become practised at this and partly because I now know where everything is kept. In the main it is due to following the same routine each day.

On arrival in the kitchen at 6.25 a.m. the first task is to switch on the gas oven to warm up in preparation for the sausages. I then turn on the hot cupboard. This takes several minutes to achieve maximum temperature. I then check the temperature of each refrigerator and freezer unit and record the result. This is checked again in the evening. Food hygiene dictates that this is carried out twice a day and it is important to know that each unit is working satisfactorily.

The main difference in the daily routine, and one which I attribute to saving five to six minutes each day, is that I follow the same pattern. If I open one of our fridges I take out everything that is required; the same goes for each cupboard. Before this I would follow a routine but this would involve revisiting each cupboard for different items. This may sound ridiculous but it works. The time saved is used to start another job and one that would have been left until after breakfast. If you can save time like this it does benefit you and the business. Working more efficiently leads to more effectiveness and can mean 20 minutes extra in the day for you personally. When we had more people working in the kitchen less was achieved and more time was wasted standing around discussing the issue of the day or gossiping.

The sausages take around 30 minutes at 180–190°C. We use a thermometer to check that the sausages have reached a safe level, over 100 degrees. The croissants are introduced to the oven at 6.45 a.m. and take 10 to 15 minutes.

In quiet times during breakfast I start to prepare the content for the following day's breakfast. Up until recently I waited to do this until breakfast had been cleared away or prepared this after lunchtime. The preparation includes making sure that you have sufficient supplies in the fridge. This task is usually completed by 9.30 a.m. and it is not something that has to be revisited until the next day.

Once each task has been completed in the kitchen, I then venture into the reception area to open up the hotel for the day. This involves turning on lights that have not been left on overnight, opening curtains, opening the breakfast room door, turning on the television in the guests' lounge and selecting a news channel, opening the office and collecting the day's newspapers from the doormat. Occasionally it involves clearing glasses and discarded litter from the bar and lounge areas. I then head back to the kitchen and begin to prepare for the first guests.

Allowing a period of 90 minutes for breakfast does give guests the opportunity to have a lie in and take breakfast. It can be annoying when a guest does not come down to breakfast if you have been waiting for them. This upset us initially. You have to remember how you behave when you stay in a hotel. Sometimes you decide to forego breakfast to stay in bed. This is usually a last-minute decision and can depend on the weather. We find that some guests delay breakfast if it is raining, cold and dark outside and prefer to stay in bed rather than face the day.

If you have regular customers you will soon pick up on their daily routine. If you only have one or two guests staying with you there is no harm in asking them if they have a preferred time for breakfast. We believe in giving our customers a choice: this is key to making them feel relaxed and at home. When we have only a couple of guests in residence or even just one we ask them what time they would like to take breakfast. If they specify 8 a.m. we offer to extend this to between 8.00 and 8.30 a.m. This gives them the scope to relax and not to feel rushed. Making your guests comfortable is another key factor in their decision whether to return. Insisting on a regimented time for breakfast will not achieve this.

During breakfast we clean and wash up as much as we can. Keeping the kitchen clean and tidy gives you more space to work in and results in less effort once breakfast is over. It is also more hygienic.

We also count the number of guests that we have already served. This helps us to plan and to ensure that we have sufficient food prepared for the rest of the session. Unless you have asked each guest to select breakfast the night before there is no way of telling exactly how much food you will need. We make an estimate based on who is saying with us. We roughly know what our regulars will have and it is then a simple case of ensuring you have enough food available for everyone.

For us, the main consideration every day is that we cook sufficient sausages in time for when breakfast begins. As sausages take up to 30 minutes to cook in the oven it can be a problem if you run out of them half way through breakfast. Defrosting frozen sausages and frying in oil takes too long and can be messy. Every other ingredient can be cooked within a few minutes.

Asking guests to select their breakfast a day in advance is not something we subscribe to. We prefer to give our guests a choice on the day. I recently stayed in a small bed-and-breakfast hotel while visiting my sister. It was a Sunday and I was the only guest staying that day. The owner checked me in and furnished me with a computer-generated menu for breakfast which had to be completed and returned before I went to bed. It didn't feel very professional; however, I understood that as a small business they probably kept a strict control on their budget and didn't wish to waste food. We do waste food at breakfast time; however, with experience we have learned to waste much less than when we first started out. The owner also informed me that breakfast on a Monday morning began at 8.30 a.m. and ended at 9.30 a.m. I had already informed him that I had an early start the next day and he set the breakfast time accordingly. The 8.30 a.m. start meant that I would leave before breakfast and that the owner would therefore not have to get up so early or prepare anything for his only guest.

While I understood his reason for this I felt aggrieved that I would miss out on breakfast. With a five-hour drive ahead breakfast was important to me. In my room I found a sign on the wall which gave the times for breakfast. The usual start time on Monday to Friday mornings was 7.30 a.m. Breakfast on Saturdays and Sundays began at 8.30 a.m. The owner had deliberately misled me to satisfy his own needs. I will not be staying there again and have already told other family members to avoid the establishment. Customer service is paramount.

When we have a guest stay on a Sunday night they are quite often the only guest staying with us. Our breakfast times are explained to each guest at check in and we have a sign in reception in case they forget. We do ask what time they have to leave in the morning and what the most appropriate time would be for them to take breakfast. More often than not they will choose the normal start time. If you are a guest it is difficult to say what time you would like breakfast the next day, unless you have an appointment. On many occasions guests have come down either earlier or later than the time they have specified. There is little point in allowing this to upset you. People change their minds, and if they are staying in a hotel they have every right to do so. They quite rightly expect the owner not to pressurise them.

Serving guests at breakfast is all about timing. You do not want to leave them waiting for over ten minutes once they have ordered. Remember how you feel if you are left waiting for your breakfast for more than ten minutes when you stay in a hotel. On the other hand, serving people too quickly will make them feel uncomfortable and rushed. If someone is in a hurry they will tell you. If not, breakfast can be a time for contemplation and reflection on the night before and the day ahead.

Business people are usually on a tight schedule. If they are working locally their time is less of an issue. Holidaymakers in the main will want to take their time. Whichever type of guests you are dealing with you must judge as best you can how much time they will need for breakfast. Do not hurry them or do things that will make them feel uncomfortable just because you want to get finished. We have had guests sit in our breakfast room for an hour after breakfast officially ended. Rather than clearing their table and asking them what time they were leaving we left them to it and worked on other tasks. When we felt that they had outstayed their welcome we asked them if they required any more tea or coffee. This is usually a good way of indicating to them that breakfast is over without resulting to rudeness.

If a guest is late for breakfast and arrives in the dining room five or ten minutes after the published time we always try to accommodate them. We allow a period of ten minutes grace for latecomers before we begin to clear up. Guests do from time to time oversleep and refusing them breakfast because they are a few minutes late will not endear you to them.

8.30–10.00 a.m.   Clean up after breakfast – kitchen and breakfast room

Again, we follow the same routine everyday. We clear the table once each guest has finished breakfast and if time allows we reset. If the breakfast room is reasonably full there is not time to do this and we are mindful of making guests feel uncomfortable.

We clear all tables and load the dishwasher. At the same time we wash up pots and pans and tidy away any reusable items. Once finished we clear the rest of the breakfast room and put away anything reusable or discard any food that is no longer of use. This includes fruit, melon, prunes, yoghurt, etc.

Once we have completed clearing away we reset the tables in the breakfast room and sweep the floor and dining chairs. We clean all of the surfaces in the kitchen and sweep the floor. All surfaces are also sprayed with anti-bacterial spray and wiped over with kitchen roll. We keep the kitchen clean and tidy at all times.

We then turn the dishwasher on and this takes approximately 90 minutes to complete its cycle. By 9.30 a.m. we are normally finished in the kitchen. If all of the guests had breakfast and departed early it is possible to finish earlier. If this happens we use the time to clean various parts of the kitchen. On rotation we thoroughly clean a different area of the kitchen each day. This includes cupboard doors, the floor, inside the oven and fridges and on top of the fridges.

9.10 a.m.   Meeting to brief cleaners

10.00–10.15 a.m. Prepare for breakfast the next day

We have often prepared the kitchen for the following day during a lull in breakfast traffic. If not completed in this time we finish off after we have cleared up.

The cleaners begin to arrive from 8.50 a.m. and we brief them for five minutes before they start. This includes giving them a list of which rooms need their attention and which guests are staying or leaving. We also let them know if any of the rooms are for double occupancy.

If a guest is staying for more than one night we change the sheets and quilt cover every other day, unless they are particularly dirty. Each room is thoroughly cleaned and towels are changed every day. We place a bottle of still water with a glass in each room. This is complimentary. The courtesy tray in each room includes tea, coffee, cartons of milk and cream, a sachet of hot chocolate and two biscuits – and of course an electric kettle and a cup and saucer!

10.15 a.m.–1.00 p.m. Morning routine

We make a list of the tasks that must be completed each day. This ensures that we do not forget anything that is crucial to the smooth running of the hotel. We do undertake other duties; however, these are not usually vital and could be executed the following day.

The daily list

1. Fridge temperatures a.m.
2. Fridge temperatures p.m.
3. Fridge content
4. Staff rota
5. E-mails
6. Breakfast room/dishwasher
7. Banking
8. End of day
9. Invoices for tomorrow
10. Post
11. Kitchen
12. Room keys
13. Lounge/bar
14. Shopping
15. Telephone usage
16. Late rooms e-mail
17. 4.00 p.m. – lights and curtains in rooms
18. List for tomorrow

Fridge temperatures a.m./p.m. and content

The fridge temperatures are checked first thing each day and again mid-afternoon. The fridge content is checked and refreshed where required either during or just after breakfast.

Staff rota

We keep a daily record of the hours each member of staff works each day. We initially asked each person to complete a timesheet. However, we soon realised that it would be much simpler for us to keep a note.

E-mails

E-mail messages are checked after breakfast and again at regular intervals throughout the day. Any booking enquiry is responded to on receipt.

Breakfast room/dishwasher

The breakfast room is reset and the dishwasher is emptied in readiness for the following morning.

Banking

We reconcile the payments received from each guest everyday. We run an end-of-day procedure on the credit card machine and this is tallied to our total for the daily revenue. We log details of each guest on our computer. This ensures we have a record of every transaction and that we can keep track of our progress. It also enables us to analyse each month and compare with previous months. It gives us an immediate picture of occupancy levels and we can check which companies stay on a frequent basis and which do not.

End of day

Reconciling revenue each day is a job that can be left until the end of the week. However, if you do so it takes longer. We find that 20 minutes each day rather than an hour or so on a Friday is more efficient.

Payments on your credit card machine must be reconciled every day and you must check that each day's takings tally with your bank statement.

Invoices for tomorrow

We prepare invoices for guests as a VAT receipt for the payments they make to us. We do this in advance as it saves time when checking guests out. If you are cooking breakfast, have a guest at reception waiting to check out and then have to write out an invoice there could be a delay. It can lead to you burning the bacon!

Post

Our post arrives between 11.30 a.m. and 12 noon. We open the post as soon as it arrives. We sort it according to urgency. Invoices are placed in a file either for urgent payment or for settlement at the end of the month. We receive at least one item of post a day containing details of items on sale to hotels. If this is of interest we keep it for reference. You never know when you might need something.

Kitchen

We clean the kitchen after breakfast each day. We mop the floor at least twice a week and whenever we feel it needs it. Fridges are cleaned out once a week. This involves taking out all of the shelves and cleaning them. The fridge content is turned over every day. However, it is essential to check sell by dates and that all items are fresh on a daily basis.

Room keys

We check that each guest has returned their room key if they have left. It is very easy to forget to ask for the key. We have had keys posted back to us from all over the globe. While we do have spare keys for each room it is annoying and inconvenient when you forget to ask and a guest takes the key with them.

We have had guests stay with us that claimed to have lost their key when they came to check out. Losing a key can have consequences. We give each guest a key to the front door and a separate key to their room. The key fob does not give any clue as to ownership just in case it is lost and found by somebody not of an honest nature. In cases where a guest says that they have lost their key we have found that informing them of the cost of replacing every lock in the hotel usually focuses their minds and the key is quickly found.

Some hotels use a security system and give each guest a fob or a code to an electronic key entry pad. If you live in the hotel this is easier to control. We have chosen not to install this system as it an additional expense and can involve changing the security number each day.

Lounge/bar

We dust the furniture and the bar/reception desk each day. We puff up cushions and generally tidy each area. Once a week we give both rooms a spring clean. The bar area doubles as our reception and as it is the first room a guest sees on arrival it is important this leaves a lasting impression.

Shopping

We shop on a Monday and a Thursday at the local supermarket. We top up on a daily basis from shops in our high street. The Monday shop sees us through to the end of the week and the Thursday shop covers the weekend.

Telephone usage

Our computer has software that logs any telephone calls made. We check whether a guest has used the telephone in their room and charge them accordingly.

Late rooms e-mail

If for any reason we find that we have a room or two available on a weekday we send an e-mail to our regular customers to let them know. We often receive cancellations. Business travellers attending a meeting can be subject to last-minute changes. Before we embarked on this we contacted each of our customers and let them know the rationale behind the system. As a result we have filled many empty rooms when guests have cancelled at the last minute. This has also resulted in less cancellation charges being made.

4.00 p.m – lights and curtains in rooms

During the winter months, as darkness falls we switch on the beside light and close the curtains in each room. When a guest arrives their room feels more welcoming and comfortable.

List for tomorrow

We keep a list of other key tasks for each day on a diary system on our computer.

Target rooms

Our daily list also carries a note of our target for occupancy for the month. To set the target we check the corresponding month for the previous year's occupancy and set a slightly higher figure.

To sell	300
Target	180
Sold to date	165
£ per room	78
Target	£14,040
Occupancy target	60%

The 'To sell' figure corresponds to the number of days in the month multiplied by the number of rooms available. We keep a running total each day of the number of rooms sold to date. Within a week of the beginning of each month we are in a position to estimate occupancy for the entire month.

Our '£ per room' figure is the yield for a room based on an average of our standard and superior tariff. This gives us a good feel for monthly turnover before we have actually reached the end of the month.

When each item on the list is completed we strike through the entry. At any given time you have an instant picture of how much work you have left to do and how much you have achieved. This also gives you an indication of how much time you will have for other activities.

On most days we have completed the morning tasks by 12 noon. This allows sufficient time to clean certain areas of the hotel not covered by the cleaners. On rotation we spring clean the ground-floor rooms. It takes two hours for one of us to clean the entire ground floor, consequently we have chosen to clean one or two rooms each day. The ground floor comprises the reception and bar area, the guests' lounge, breakfast room and a public convenience. It also includes two hallways and the kitchen. We also vacuum and mop the floors and clean the public toilets.

2.30–7.00 p.m.   Afternoon routine

Any task not completed from the morning list is carried out during the afternoon. Our cleaners leave at 1.00 p.m. and on the odd occasion they have not been able to fulfil their duties we undertake to complete them. This sometimes happens when a guest is late checking out or if they forget to clean a room.

If time allows we use the early afternoon to undertake any work in the garden or maintenance to the building. During the week guests rarely arrive before 4.30 p.m. This allows time to mow the lawn or to clean up any litter or debris fallen from the trees in our grounds.

At weekends we usually finish work by lunchtime and take the afternoon off. Weekend guests arrive mid-afternoon or later. We always ask weekend guests when they are making the booking for an approximate time of arrival Occasionally they check in mid-morning and during the summer months we attract wedding guests who nearly always check in before attending the wedding.

The afternoon schedule does largely depend on the season. Not much gardening is done over the November to February period, though we do monitor the grounds and clear any debris. We check our gutters and remove any blockages. If we spot any maintenance of the building that needs our attention we plan any action to be taken and make preparations for when repairs can be made. Again this is largely at the mercy of the weather.

Marketing is also something that we work on during the quiet early afternoon. We often trawl the internet and search for websites advertising hotels. We keep an eye on our competition and make searches to ensure that our hotel appears in the same places as other local hotels.

4.30 p.m.–8.00 p.m.   Guests arrive to check in

By 4.30 p.m. our guests begin to arrive and much of the early evening is spent checking guests in and chatting to them. Many will ask for information about the local facilities. This can be anything from the nearest restaurant or pub to the local cinema. Over time we have been asked for all sorts of information and now we are prepared for most questions. Guests expect you to have the answer to everything and it is fun and rewarding to be in a position to help them. When you do this it leaves a lasting impression.

During the winter months we close the curtains and turn on the lights inside and out. We keep the front and back door locked most of the time. If a guest is leaving we try to be available to open doors for them and wish them a safe onward journey.

If guests are checking in we can see them arrive if they leave their vehicle in our car park and we can greet them at the door. If they ring on the front door bell we answer this as quickly as possible. Leaving a guest in the rain or cold for too long is not to be recommended. Guests are often surprised that our door is locked. They expect a hotel to be open at all times and to be able to walk straight in. However, we prefer to keep the doors locked for security. If we are in our house it is not always possible to keep an eye on the hotel, even though we have a CCTV system.

Guests also drink at our bar in the early part of the evening, before venturing out to visit a local restaurant. We carry details of each of the closest restaurants to the hotel and include menus in each room and on reception. We have eaten in most of the restaurants and feel confident in recommending them. We ask guests for their feedback as this also gives us a second opinion. We don't have the time to eat out that often so it is important for us to gain a guest's opinion from time to time.

At check-in we inform guests of any house rules and the time for breakfast. We ask any guest that is staying for the first time whether they have an early start in the morning. This helps us to judge what to expect and if we will be busy at 7.00 a.m. or if guests will be down later. If the opportunity arises we discuss their plans. This is very useful at weekends if guests are going out to functions. If they are not planning to be back before midnight it allows us to close up and go to bed earlier. Information, as they say, is power!

7.00 p.m. Monday to Thursday – evening receptionist arrives

Our evening receptionist arrives at 7.00 p.m. and she looks after the hotel for us until she closes up at 11.00 p.m. As we are open all year round we experience very few quiet periods and we find that by 7.00 p.m. we are pretty much exhausted. Having Monday to Thursday evenings off has become of great value to us. If our receptionist is unable to work we find that closing up at 11.00 p.m. and being up the next day at 5.54 a.m. is too tiring. An evening receptionist is a luxury for a small hotel; however, we have to balance our work and rest time and we have found that this suits us well. It is also of value to have a change of personnel in the evening and guests appreciate being looked after by a different face.

As we do not live on the premises it becomes more of a chore to service our guests if we are not readily available. If you live on site it is easier and quicker to attend to a guest.

11.00 p.m.   Hotel locked down for the night

We turn off the outside lights and some of the non-essential internal lights. We leave lights on in our hallway and stairs. Now and again guests take it upon themselves to turn these lights off – some people just can't help themselves and instinctively turn off lights as they would do at home. If they are staying for more than one night we point out to them, politely, that the lights are left on for security.

We also check that the front and back doors have not been left open and we ensure that all fire doors are closed.

We choose to close our bar at 11 p.m. We have discussed closing up earlier and do so if all of our guests are coming back late. However, we feel that we should offer similar facilities to those at larger hotels.

Guests sometimes lock themselves out of the hotel by forgetting to take their key with them and wake us up in the small hours. Now and again we have a guest who wants a nightcap after the bar is closed. While this can be annoying, it will happen. It is your attitude towards the guest and how you deal with them that can make all the difference. We never show the guest how much they have inconvenienced us.

Our story from the beginning

The day of the move

Moving house for any reason is a stressful exercise. Doing so to make a major lifestyle change and move away from an area you feel at home with increases the levels of stress. It is also exhilarating.

Our move ran relatively smoothly until the solicitors started to question whether the necessary funds had arrived or not. We had to endure an anxious period of a couple of hours while each solicitor decided who was to blame for a breakdown in communication. There was nothing much we could do other than wait for a telephone call.

Once the financial transactions were confirmed we sat in our car outside our old house and just looked at each other for a while. It took a few minutes for the enormity of our situation to sink in. Life was about to change for good. We felt excited. There is so much to consider when taking such a big step. Will the children settle into their new environment? Will we be any good at running a hotel? What will our new house be like to live in? We had done our homework and found out as much as we could about the location and the surrounding environment but we were still anxious.

On the day we moved it was a beautiful warm summer's day in June. Our children were staying with their grandparents and were due to join us in a couple of days. We chose not to put them through too much upheaval and to allow ourselves time to pack and to move our belongings to our new abode.

Our journey was interrupted by telephone calls from removal men, solicitors, outgoing hotel owners and estate agents. They didn't leave us much time to dwell on what lay ahead. We started out at 2 p.m. and soon became ensnared by the M25. When we reached our destination after nearly three hours, we were exhausted, yet we still had the joys of unpacking and settling in to our new home. We also had two guests already in residence and a further two couples due at any time.

With our belongings dumped by our removal men all over our new house and in no particular order, and our garden furniture left in a huge pile on the hotel lawn, all we really wanted to do was run away and hide. It was a very warm day and we set about clearing the hotel lawn as a priority. Our first guests arrived at 6 p.m., just half an hour after the previous owners had left the scene and about five minutes after the last remnants of our garden furniture and been deposited in our barn (some of which I have not set eyes on again to this day!).

The day of arrival was always going to be tough and it took real determination to keep going and to act professionally when our guests arrived. The thought that helped the most was that things could only get better. We both longed for the day when we felt comfortable and at home. On the first day you are the farthest from this point as you can possibly be.

Bedtime could not come soon enough. The previous owners had left us a full list of what we needed to do each day. This included everything from opening up in the morning to closing up each night. This didn't help us sleep that well, but it was an excellent document to refer to in our first week.

By the time we closed up the hotel that evening we were more than ready for bed. Our new house was still in chaos but we were prepared for the challenge ahead. Our dream had become a reality.

Our first two days

The yearning to feel comfortable with what we were doing did not subside for several weeks. The feeling that we had made the right move didn't establish itself for many months. My recollection of the first two days is more than a little hazy. In fact the only day that is memorable to me is the day that we arrived.

The hotel was full on day two. Only one couple that stayed on our first night stayed for the second. We had nine couples arriving and 20 breakfasts to prepare for. We had a stock list to check through and a fixtures and fittings inventory to reconcile. We had new staff to meet. We had met just two of the cleaners before our arrival; day one introduced us to our cook and two of our waitresses. It then dawned on us that our staff would be relying on us to know what to do and how to run a hotel. They had not been party to any of our conversations with the outgoing owners and knew nothing of our background.

So here we were, responsible for a Grade 2 listed building of historical value, a hotel with 20 paying guests, five staff in need of instruction and our children about to arrive to check out their new home. In the cold light of day our decision to uproot was beginning to feel a little misguided. This is where all of the preparation becomes significant. You have to be ready to hit the ground running. There is nobody else around to make decisions for you. You have to support each other and communicate if you are going to pull through. Above all else, you have to work hard and rely on your customers for your living.

The reason I do not remember much after the first day is entirely due to an accident, which befell me in mid-August, just six weeks after we took over. It was a Sunday morning and I had been preparing breakfast for 20 guests. I had to return to our house to change as apparently I had spilt something on my clothing. I woke up in hospital on Wednesday morning surrounded by nurses and other patients. Retrograde amnesia put paid to any memory I have of the first six weeks, other than the day we arrived. Our bookings diary and account records show that we achieved 62% occupancy and that 194 guests stayed with us in August. Everything else that took place in those first six weeks is not even a blur.

It is not really an incident that I like to discuss and I prefer to look forward. It is, however, an example of what can happen to anyone at any moment. It also demonstrates that running a hotel relies on the owners being fit and healthy, and therefore available at all times.

On the day in question I, for some unknown reason, collided with a low beam in the bedroom of our house. We live in a barn conversion and our bedroom is located in the roof. We have two low beams across the room and these are a hazard to anyone over 5 ft 4 in tall. For me at 6 ft the hazard was almost a fatal obstacle.

I had fractured my skull and my eye socket. The collision had sent me crashing to the floor and en route my eye met with a clotheshorse. The impact resulted in two micro brain haemorrhages, which in turn caused a seizure. I was discovered walking around covered in blood. Although I had been conscious throughout my three days in hospital I have no recollection of this or of the accident.

When I came to my senses a nurse asked me if I knew where I was and where I lived. I can remember at the time thinking that these were very strange questions as it was obvious I was in hospital and that I lived in Watford. The nurse then asked what I did for a living. I replied that I organised events. I had no idea that I was now a hotelier or that I lived in Chipping Sodbury. It was only when I was shown a photograph of the hotel that I had any recollection of our new life. I left hospital after a week with no outward signs that anything had happened to me at all. This is one of the drawbacks to a fractured skull – it is not a condition that can be treated by anything other than rest. There is no bandage or plaster cast to indicate that you are not well, and when you work for yourself, no chance at all of any rest.

When you run a small hotel the business relies on its owners being available and in service at all times. You must consider how you would be able to function if you met with a similar crisis and one that interrupts your ability to run your business. We were insured for business continuity and for critical illness, but neither policy included cover for my accident or for the time I spent in hospital.

My in-laws took over the hotel while I was in hospital and stayed for a further two weeks as I recovered. Our staff looked after breakfast time and the cleaning. My father-in-law kept watch and took responsibility for registering guests and taking their money. My wife shopped for and monitored the hotel supplies and paid the staff. I sat in hospital oblivious to all of this. The painkillers and anti-seizure drugs ensured I relaxed and did not worry about the business. Not remembering that I ran a hotel helped as well!

My in-laws had very little business experience and had certainly never run a hotel before. This first exposure to the hotel trade stood them in good stead for when I reacted to the anti-seizure drugs and ended up back in hospital for a further two weeks. The reaction to the drugs took hold over a period of two months and by mid-October my ability to function effectively disappeared altogether. After two weeks of continual tests the doctors agreed with my self-diagnosis and confirmed that I had had an allergic reaction to the drugs that they prescribed which caused a rare condition related to septicaemia. I spent a further two weeks in hospital in an isolation unit. At last I had two weeks holiday!

Over the next four weeks my in-laws, now experienced in hotel management, took over the day-to-day running of the hotel. Together with our staff they kept the business ticking over.

The entire episode accounted for nearly five of our first six months in business and seriously affected our ability to run the hotel effectively. It delayed our induction into the hotel trade. As a consequence it took us much longer to gain an understanding of the occupancy trends and of how to market the hotel to potential customers.

My in-laws did a sterling job for us but they could do little more than keep the hotel ticking over. It was only after we had managed the hotel over the corresponding period the following year that we were in a position to calculate the financial implications of my accident. In 2007 our revenue increased over the same four-month period by £17.5k. We are still recovering and expect this to take another year or so.

6–12 months

We gradually increased our occupancy levels and an improvement in our weekend trade indicated that we were making progress. Our location dictates the level of weekend business. November through to March is much quieter at weekends and we only have one or two bookings for each Friday and Saturday. Our weekday occupancy is consistent all year round.

Our occupancy level for 2007 was 67%. For the period between May and October we achieved 70%. We were full most weekends with the exception of

Sundays. It is clear that Sundays will always be quiet. Every now and then we have a Sunday that takes us by surprise and we are full. However, this is the exception as opposed to the rule. Weekend guests stay on either Friday or Saturday, or both. Very few extend their stay to a Sunday.

When we prepared our business plan our initial targets were to maintain and build upon the level of trade from business customers and to increase the weekend visitors. We also intended to promote the hotel to tourists. It was clear from the hotel records that very few tourists had booked more than the odd day here and there.

After a year of ownership we now know that our location is not popular with tourists. We are on the edge of the Cotswolds and have major competition in every direction. Our town is a place which attracts the afternoon tourist paying a quick visit en route to other tourist traps. We have established that our market is firmly with the local trade and this is where we target most of our marketing budget.

It would be tempting to attack the tourist market but this would need a huge marketing campaign with no guarantee of success.

After 12 months we began to feel more at home. Up until then it felt as if we had made a temporary move and did not fit into the local community. We live in a beautiful medieval town and we are surrounded by history dating back to the ninth and tenth centuries. Some of the local families also date back to this period. In our first few months we constantly had the feeling, when we walked along the high street, that we were staying in the town as holidaymakers, not because we spent all day lounging in our garden but from the feel and look of the town, and because we had taken quite a few holidays in the Cotswolds prior to our arrival.

Lots of unfamiliar things happen to us on a daily basis. It has taken 18 months to experience most things but even so something turns up now and again which surprises us.

We are reasonably well known in the town. Our marketing locally, combined with the fact that we visit other businesses in our street on a regular basis, has helped us to establish our weekend trade. It does take time to build up and you need to be patient. Word of mouth is the best and least expensive form of advertising. If our customers are happy with their stay here they will tell other people and they will stay again themselves.

We have also parted company with some of our staff over the first year or so. Most have left to take a full-time position as a career move. We have had to dismiss one employee. This is not something we took lightly and we only decided on this after consultation with the company which looks after our PAYE. It is always advisable to seek a second opinion and check your legal rights, and those of the employee in question, before taking action. Thankfully the employee we dismissed didn't leave us with any choice.

We have taken on new people and still have three of the original team working with us. We also have a member of staff working for us that we employed over a year ago.

When a member of your team leaves it does create a problem for you. Finding a suitable replacement is not that straightforward. We have been lucky with the choices we made.

The source of our weekday trade has changed. When we first started we had a couple of regular customers who stayed with us on a weekly basis. We inherited these customers from the previous owners. At present we have over ten regular guests who stay for more than one night a week every week. When the course of their business takes them away from us they are often replaced by one of their colleagues.

At the start we had several new guests stay with us every week. Many of these are now our regulars. We feel that this is an indication that we are running the hotel to the liking of our customers and as a result they are happy to return. Our location also plays a major role in this.

18 months later – what we think now

Over the course of the first year we have both experienced serious doubts over the move. We miss our friends and it was more difficult to visit family. When we arrived we didn't know anybody living in the town and our neighbours were all strangers. Our eldest child had to start at a new school and he missed his friends too. This was of deep concern as our children's happiness is more important than anything that affects us.

We knew nothing about running a hotel. As someone that worked from home I had become accustomed to working alone. We were now surrounded by staff relying on us to pay them.

We often discussed how we felt and there were moments we considered selling up. We still think about this occasionally but much less frequently than before. Thinking about selling has become something that is only considered when we are analysing our financial circumstances. This is healthy. There is little point in persevering when you have nothing to gain.

So how do we feel now? We still have a few doubts now and again but not over where we live. This is more based upon our bank balance and how hard we have to work.

Rising early each morning is much easier now, even when it is dark and cold for five months of the year. It has become a way of life. When we discuss our situation we always consider our finances rather than our location. We also think back to our previous lifestyle and contemplate what we would do to earn a living if we didn't run a hotel.

We are comfortable with running the hotel. We are still learning and each day is an adventure. We are happy with where we live and more importantly our children are happy too. We have kept in touch with our old friends and they do pay us a visit from time to time. We know all of our neighbours and have made friends with other local business owners.

In our first year we were confronted with a different problem to solve on most days of the week. Now we have overcome most of these problems and know how to deal with them and how to prepare for them.

We are looking to improve upon our occupancy levels and believe that the hard work that we have already put in will help us to achieve this.

Our only real concern is our financial situation. The mortgage that we first arranged was pretty much the only option available to us at the time. The lender had very little experience in the commercial sector and had advised us that we were their first customers in the leisure industry in many years. Our plan had always included the probability of looking to refinance at some stage. This is something that we are now involved with. We explored refinancing with our existing lender; however, the financial climate was such that this was not something that interested them.

The original deal was the best that we could have hoped for bearing in mind the amount of capital we were looking to raise. We will always be thankful to the lender for turning our dream into a reality. It is now time to make the next move to ensure our long-term security.

We have been surprised at how defensive we have become of our business. It must indicate that we are happy if we are so protective over a chunk of real estate.

Analysing your situation constantly will ensure that when you need to make a move you are ready to do so and for the right reasons.

Appendix:
An A–Z of practical advice

Contents

Accounting

Answering the telephone

Banking

Be prepared to do everything yourself!

Booking procedures

Cancellation policy

Complaints

Events

Housekeeping

How to deal with customers

How to deal with sales calls

Insurance

Maintenance

Marketing

Practical advice

Professional fees and licensing

Provisions

Research

Security

Smoking

Staff

Suppliers

Utilities

VAT

Your environment

Your website

Accounting

Keeping a record of your income and outgoings is fundamental even if you have no previous accounting experience. You will need an accountant to prepare your annual accounts and this must be factored into your budget. Your business bank will also offer to supply you with accounting software, either as an additional expense or as part of your agreement.

Keeping a daily tally of your income has two major plus points. It makes you feel good when you add up how much money you have taken and, more importantly, it gives you an instant picture of how well you are doing. It allows you to produce a weekly and monthly report on revenue.

Many of the costs associated with running a hotel do not attract VAT as they are zero rated. If you are VAT registered this will affect you as when you come to claim back VAT this will affect the amount of VAT you have to pay. Investigate this with your VAT office and ask them to send you details of the different schemes they run for small businesses. This information is also available online.

In Note 1 at the end of the A–Z you will find a list of the main expenditure items that you will have to account for. We prepare our management accounts at the end of each month and produce a report detailing the profit (or loss) that we have made.

We pay invoices at different times of the month depending on our cash flow. We pay for critical supplies at the beginning of each month or on delivery. We keep a file of all invoices received and prioritise them. We only pay other suppliers when we are certain we have the funds available.

Keep an eye on your business account. Check that you have received all revenue from guests and that all of your key payments have been made. We check our account online most days.

If you record your income and expenditure in this way it will make life easier for you at the end of each financial year. It will also reduce your costs, as your accountant will have less to do. It will also give you an instant and up-to-date record of your financial position. This is crucial in your first couple of years of hotel ownership.

Answering the telephone

Politeness and professionalism are the keys. You never know before the caller speaks whether they are a potential customer or an annoying call centre sales person.

Never sound miserable even if you are. Setting a good impression is vital if you are to attract new custom.

If the caller is trying to sell you something, be polite, find out what it is they are selling and ask them to send you details. Do not waste time on this type of call. If the caller is trying to make a fast buck and requires an immediate decision they are not to be trusted and should be dealt with quickly. But do remember that they may have a product that could be of use to you in the future.

Try not to miss a call or let the telephone ring off before you reach it. Again, it could be someone wishing to book a room. If you do have to leave the telephone unattended for any reason ensure that you have voicemail or an answering machine in place to record the call. When you do have calls of this nature call them back as soon as you can. If they are looking to book a room they might find an alternative before you can reach them.

Banking

Always run your end-of-day procedure through your credit card processing machine as soon as your last guest has checked out and settled their bill.

Reconcile this with your invoices or receipts to check that all of the guests that should have paid have done so. This does sound obvious but you will at some stage forget that a guest is checking out and needs to pay.

If a customer pays by cheque you must bank this as soon as you can (although in 18 months we have received only five cheques in payment for a room). Remember that cheques do take time to clear.

When you process customers' payments you must keep a copy of any invoice and if they have settled their bill by credit or debit card you should also retain the merchant copy of the card receipt generated by your card processing terminal.

Keeping a copy of each payment record will enable you to reconcile your receipts at the end of a given period. We also record our payments in a spreadsheet and add any new receipts on a daily basis. This gives us an up-to-date record and allows us to check any discrepancies.

If a guest pays in cash it is your decision as to how to account for this. We record all payments using the same method. Cash is treated in the same way as any other type of payment. The only exception to this is that we do not pay cash into our bank unless it is essential do so. We tend to keep hold of any cash payments and use them to pay for supplies instead of using our debit card.

Be prepared to do everything yourself!

If your budget is tight you will not always be in a position to hire a tradesman to carry out a repair or to hire sufficient staff to cover every duty. Your staff will sometimes take a day or two off sick or go on holiday. It is possible to hire personnel to cover when you are short of staff but this can be expensive.

You might run out of linen. You might be called upon to change a light bulb or to replace a fuse. There is an endless list of similar tasks than can occur at any time. It will not always be possible to find someone willing or available to help you out.

You must be adaptable and willing to undertake any task. Over the course of our first 18 months we have: cleaned the rooms when the cleaner is unavailable; waited on tables when the waitress has called in sick; washed and ironed table linen when we have run out; repaired all manner of fixtures and fittings such as door locks, shower heads, shower curtains and chipped baths; taken over cooking the breakfast; unblocked the guttering; cleared fallen branches from the garden; redecorated a guest bedroom; laundered guests' underwear; and the list goes on.

Booking procedures

When you receive a booking you must record this in your diary and make a note against the entry of the following: name of guest, single or double occupancy, guest's telephone number, name and telephone number of the person booking the room if different from that of the guest, duration of stay, a credit or debit card number, its expiry date and three-digit security number and the price agreed for the room. You might also ask for an expected time of arrival. This is useful if the guest has indicated they will be arriving late or during the evening.

If your hotel offers full or half board you may also ask if any of the guests in the party have any special dietary requirements or are vegetarian.

When taking a booking by telephone you should ask the caller to confirm the booking in writing either by fax or by e-mail. In some circumstances the guest will write to you to confirm. We make a note against the diary entry that the caller will confirm and by which method. When the confirmation arrives we also make a note. This helps us to double check that a booking has been confirmed. This is important. If a confirmation does not materialise you might find that a guest has changed their mind and has not let you know.

At the end of any such telephone call you should reconfirm the details of the booking and in particular the date before you end the call. Be clear and precise when confirming the date as you may have misheard the caller's initial request. This avoids any misunderstandings at a later stage of the booking procedure.

When a confirmation is received you should respond and acknowledge the booking as soon as it is received. Note 2 at the end of the A–Z gives you an example of our response. This should include the date of the guest's stay, the duration of the stay and the type of room. It should detail the tariff and whether the price includes VAT, breakfast or full/half board. It must also explain your cancellation policy and any relevant travel information such as directions and the exact location of your hotel.

We include details of any special offers or services that we provide and mention that our hotel has a customer car park. In addition we make our guests aware that the hotel is entirely non-smoking in accordance with the legislation effective from 1 July 2007.

The most essential piece of data in your booking confirmation is arguably your cancellation policy.

When checking a guest into your hotel you must ask them to complete a registration card before handing them their room key and giving them information about the hotel This must include: the guest's name; their home address; their company name (if on business); telephone number; arrival date; departure date; payment method, i.e. card/cash/cheque; card number and expiry date; car registration number (if parked in hotel car park); customer's signature.

If the guest has travelled from overseas on a visit to the UK you must also record their passport number and their next destination. This is a legal requirement and you must keep the record for a period of five years (or the period specified by law at the time of the booking).

All of this data is of benefit to you as a hotelier. We keep a record of all of the information captured. This helps us to identify the demographics of our customers and to plan our marketing activity accordingly. You should note that there are data protection laws and you should study these to understand the legal requirements in respect of the use of personal data. We do not share our data with any third party and we do not send blanket advertising messages to our customers unless they have agreed to receive these. However, we do send Christmas cards to all regular customers.

You must be wary and pay specific attention to the privacy of each guest. You must consider this particularly for any female guest staying with you or families with young children. If the female guest is travelling alone you should not let other guests know that this is the case and you should not give out her room number to anyone without first discussing this with the guest. You should also consider if it is a security risk to place a female guest in a ground floor room.

You should not discuss whether a guest is staying with you or give any personal information to a third party unless you are absolutely certain that the guest is happy for you to do this.

Most hotels ask guests for a credit or debit card at registration to secure the booking. Many take a 'swipe' of the customer card as security. When you run your own hotel it is your decision whether to do this or not. We do not ask our regular customers for this information. If they have stayed with us before we already have this data anyway. If the guest is staying for the first time we will have already asked them for this information at the time of the booking.

Cancellation policy

It is your decision over how long you set your notice period for a guest to cancel their booking before making a cancellation charge. Our notice period is 24 hours. In certain circumstances we increase this to 36 or even 48 hours. We do this if we have a demand for rooms at a particular time of year and we know that the hotel will be full.

If a guest cancels a room after the time you have set for them to give notice, it is your decision on whether to make a cancellation charge. This might depend on the reason for the cancellation. They may have been taken ill or had an unforeseen problem which has delayed them unavoidably.

If your hotel is full and you could have let their room to another guest it will be an easier decision to make. It would be unfair of a guest to expect you to waive the cancellation fee if you could have re-let the room to somebody else had they given you more warning.

If a guest cancels and you re-let the room you should not charge a cancellation fee. If the guest has guaranteed the booking by credit or debit card and have cancelled or not appeared and haven't let you know then it is possible to process their card in the normal way and take payment. You must check with your card supplier which types of card this to applies. With some it is not possible to process a cancellation payment.

If your guest has cancelled and guaranteed the booking by card you should first ask them if it is acceptable to take payment from the card before processing this.

If the cancellation is received from a regular customer you must decide whether it is in your best interests to ask for payment. You must consider if making a charge will upset them to the extent that they will not re-book in the future.

Complaints

Stay calm and try not to take it personally! If you do receive a complaint you must deal with it, learn from the experience and move on. If the hotel is being run professionally and you are providing an excellent service to your customers you will receive very few complaints.

Examine the reasons why the customer has complained and what you could and should have done differently. If the guest is acting unreasonably and the complaint is unfounded you should still be polite and helpful in your response. There is no point in upsetting the guest any further and you may find that they become more reasonable when they see that you are trying to resolve any problem that they have had.

We have received a couple of complaints in our time and both have been in our opinion unreasonable. One guest asked us if we would record a sporting event for him to watch the next morning. The event took place in the middle of the night. He had already left for an evening out when we received his message and could not reach him to let him know that our video recorder was malfunctioning and that we would not be able to meet his request. His e-mail complaining of his outrage at missing the event was a little over the top. His main concern centred on the fact that he had missed the live action, and that he didn't feel that watching the highlights or reading the result in the newspaper were satisfactory substitutes.

It is difficult to reply to such a complaint. You really want to say what you feel and you question if the complaint is valid based on the importance of the event that the customer had missed. In hindsight we could have done more. If we received a similar request today we would do everything in our power to meet this. If this involved borrowing a video or asking a neighbour for help, so be it. A satisfied customer will come back.

We also had a complaint from a customer who did not like their room. In fact this has happened a few times. Customers have on occasion asked us if they could change rooms. This usually takes place just after they have checked in. If we can change the room we do so. The first complaint of this nature was made by a guest who didn't like the beam supporting the ceiling in their room. They had not stayed in such an old building before and felt uncomfortable and concerned that they might bump their head. They did actually say that they liked the rest of the room and asked if we could remove the beam! Other customers have asked to move because they wanted a room at the back of the hotel or on the top floor.

By helping with such requests, you demonstrate that the comfort of your guests is your priority. If they are a regular customer you should make a note of their likes and dislikes and apply this to the next time that they stay.

Events

If your hotel has sufficient facilities to host events you must first decide if you have the necessary experience to be in a position to offer customers a professional service. You must also consider the type of events you would feel most comfortable with and which would most suit your facilities.

Events are notoriously difficult to get right. Good communication and organisational skills are essential as is a meticulous eye for detail. Even if you have agreed just to let a particular function room out without any extra services, you will be expected to provide more than this. People attending the event will judge you on the success of the event, even if you have had little to do with the organisation.

Customers who book an event with you will expect and are entitled to your full attention. They will make additional demands upon you before and during their event.

If you are buying a hotel and its success depends on event trade you must decide if running events is your forte. If you are certain this is something that is for you then you must investigate this further and find out exactly what is involved before you make any commitment.

If your hotel is small and has limited facilities for functions, running events will be much more of a challenge. You might let your dining room out during the day for small conferences or meetings or even for wedding breakfasts. It might be possible to host wedding receptions if you have an area suitable for this.

Before we took over our hotel we envisaged running all manner of events. The grounds were suitable for a small marquee and the ground floor space, we thought, would be ideal for smaller functions.

In our first 18 months we have organised a wedding (50 guests), three funeral receptions, various meetings and training courses and two whisky-tasting evenings.

These have served to teach us the capacity of our hotel to host such events and our ability and willingness to offer this type of service.

The events have all been exceptionally hard work. They have been rewarding, not always financially but in being able to provide good customer service and executing successful events for our guests.

We have also viewed each event as an integral part of our marketing campaign. If you host events and the customer is happy they will tell their friends about you and this will lead to future business.

If you are buying a hotel which heavily relies on event business then you must be an experienced event organiser or have access to staff that have a proven track record in this market.

Our hotel is not really suitable for events attended by more than 50 guests. We do not turn event business away but we do examine in depth the reasons for hosting an event before we undertake to organise it. The financial reasons are not the principle concern. It is whether you can satisfy your customers' expectations that is of paramount importance. If you make mistakes and upset the customer you risk your reputation, not just as an event venue but also as a hotel. Additionally you risk not being paid in full.

Housekeeping

Your principle concern as a hotelier is the welfare and comfort of your guests. They expect a certain standard of service, however much they pay for their room.

Your hotel must be clean and presentable at all times, inside and out. Bed linen must be clean. Table linen, cutlery and crockery must be clean. Bathrooms and towels must be clean and fresh. Carpets and flooring should be spotless.

The hotel reception gives each guest a first impression. You must have a clutter-free and fragrant-smelling reception area. It must be warm, airy and welcoming. It must be dust- and litter-free. All reception rooms or areas should be the same.

The staff working in the hotel must be aware of your standards and what you expect from them. Do not assume that they think in the same way as you.

You must keep a close eye on your hotel and continually assess its state of readiness to except guests. Put yourself in your guests' shoes and decide if you would be happy to stay in your own hotel.

Check the repair of your bed linen and towels on a weekly basis. Ask your cleaning personnel to report any wear or tear. Make repairs and replacements immediately or as soon as your budget allows.

How to deal with customers

The way in which you greet your customers and communicate with them during their stay will also help determine if they return in the future.

They are your guests and you must treat them all equally. It doesn't take much effort, if any at all, to be polite and courteous at all times. You will derive pleasure from the response you receive from your customers if you are always keen and willing to assist them.

You should go out of your way to satisfy any of their requests. We look upon this as a challenge. You never know what a guest is going to ask you for – in most cases they will be looking for nothing more than an iron and ironing board, or they will have forgotten their toothbrush or razor. They will ask for the number of a local taxi company or for a recommendation of a restaurant. These requests are all relatively easy to fulfil and will take just a few moments of your time.

We were recently asked for a comb. This was a first. My initial reaction to our waitress when she informed me that a customer having breakfast had asked for this was surprise. I have very little hair and have no use of a comb and our waitress had only a hairbrush. While it would have been easy to tell the guests we could not help we had a comb at home and a couple of minutes later the customer's request was met.

We receive booking enquires by telephone, e-mail, post and at the front door. We deal with each request in the same way. By being consistent we ensure that every enquirer leaves with a good impression and will recommend us to others.

We enjoy being friendly. When you run your own business you can afford to be and at the same time you can't afford not to be.

How to deal with sales calls

You should always be polite when taking a telephone call or answering the front door. You never know when a sales call will result in something being of interest or of use to you. The sales person, or their family or friends, may even be a future guest in your hotel.

In time you will recognise this type of call as soon as you answer the telephone or door. This will allow you to deal with it appropriately. Try not to waste too much time talking to sales people. Ask them to send you their details and let them know that you will call them if you decide to make a purchase. This will save you hours of your time over the course of a year.

Insurance

You must shop around for the best possible deal. All buildings and business insurance is pretty standard and must cover the minimum legal requirements for owning and running a hotel.

Compare the quotes that you receive and make a note of what items are included or missing from each. If there is an item not included and it appears to be a crucial element ask the insurance company why it is missing.

Some insurance companies will offer you a deal with a fixed price for a couple of years. They might also allow you to settle the premium over a period of time. If this is an option you should be able to arrange this facility without having to pay an unreasonable amount of interest.

You must factor your insurance premium into your budget and be aware of when your renewal is due.

Maintenance

Your hotel will show signs of wear and tear. Having people stay in your hotel makes this unavoidable. Guests do not pay the same care and attention when staying in a hotel as they would do in their own home. Do not take this personally – it is just human nature.

At first we were annoyed by every slight paint chip or mark on the wall. It is not possible to repaint walls and paintwork every day. However, you must focus on any major repair or maintenance that does require attention, especially if it is a problem that will worsen or be of danger to your guests or staff if it is left.

Your guests will not notice if there is a small scuffmark on the wall or if the outside window frame needs some attention. If they do notice they will not view this with the same concern as you do.

If you do repair something or undertake some maintenance, keep a record of when you do so and make a note of when it will next require your attention. If you work proactively it will save you money and will avoid any major repair bills in the future.

Maintenance can cover anything that is subject to wear and tear. This can include the fabric of the building and any of the fixtures and fittings.

Marketing

How to advertise your hotel to potential customers is one of the most difficult aspects of running a small business. Your budget will not stretch to everything you would like to be involved with. You will be constantly bombarded with 'unbeatable' opportunities to increase your occupancy levels.

There are literally hundreds of online websites purporting to be the best vehicle for advertising your hotel. There are fewer publications available nowadays as print advertising struggles to compete with the internet.

You must decide what type of marketing will be the most cost-effective for you and at the same time produce the best results. The previous owners may have discovered the perfect formula and it could be a simple case of continuing with their campaign. If not you must research your area and decide who your target audience is and how to reach them.

We spend a large percentage of our marketing budget advertising locally. This is inexpensive and we know that it reaches its target.

It is tempting to advertise online with some of the major leisure industry organisations. We spent 40% of our budget in the first year in this way and will not be doing so again. It is not wise or of value to place all of your eggs in one basket.

By researching your competitors you can discover quickly where they advertise. If they continue to advertise in this way it is fairly safe to reason that their campaign is paying dividends.

Don't jump in with both feet when you receive an offer to advertise. Find out as much as you can about the company making the offer and how they operate. Ask them for proof of previous success in your area and take your time in making a decision. Do not be tempted by an offer which sounds too good to be true – it probably will be.

Practical advice

Never rush into a decision – always consider your options, examine all possible resolutions and then give yourself a day or two to think about the action required before taking any steps. We have found this to be the best way to avoid making rash decisions which can be expensive and can leave you wishing you had not acted so hastily.

I always give myself a pep talk before making a decision and I try to discuss the issue with my partner. I tell myself to wait until tomorrow – the problem may resolve itself without my intervention.

This can apply to anything connected with the day-to-day running of the hotel, from the smallest of problems to major incidents.

You will receive calls asking you to subscribe to the latest online advertising website, a snip at only £199 per year. You will have a fault with your telephone system or your computer or your washing machine or your fridge which, according to your supplier, can only be resolved if they send out a service engineer for a call-out charge of £116 plus £90 per hour.

Your staff will tell you something needs to be replaced or you will consider replacing something just to have a new appliance or piece of furniture. You will take a dislike to certain areas of the hotel or its content and desperately want to make changes.

These types of issue occur every day. If you agreed to advertise, replace, fix or purchase everything offered to you or desired by you, you will soon find yourselves in financial difficulty.

The best piece of advice I can give you is to take a chill pill, relax, don't make rash judgements, think about it and make considered decisions only once you have explored all possibilities.

You will experience days when you receive several cancellations for bookings within a couple of hours. This will make you wonder what you have done to make people cancel. This isn't a bad thing as you should be continually examining and re-examining how you approach things. However, if you are doing most things the right way then your cancellations will be nothing more than coincidence.

I have found that cancellations sometimes come in small batches of two or three and never more than four in any one day. These are usually closely followed by additional bookings from other sources. Your disappointment and doubt is then replaced by a warmer feeling! Business people change their plans frequently. Tourists very rarely cancel unless they have a serious reason to do so. Whatever the reason, it is doubtful that is has anything to do with your hotel. So stop worrying.

Professional fees and licensing

To run a hotel you will need various licences. These include a Performing Rights Society Music Certificate, a personal licence to sell alcohol, a premises licence, a TV licence and a Foundation Certificate in Food Hygiene.

You will also incur certain annual charges for professional services. These include portable appliance testing, fire security maintenance and gas safety.

If you run events and these take place in the grounds of your hotel you may also need to apply for a temporary event notice. For details of how to apply you should contact your local council.

Your accountant will also expect to be paid for their professional services and if you have a hotel rating this will also incur a charge.

Provisions

Whatever your financial position you must ensure that you are always in a position to purchase provisions. Even when your budget is tight and you need to spend money in other areas, the supply of food and drink should be your first concern.

Your guests have to be fed and watered every day. You must not run out of food supplies and this is crucial if you are to provide your customers with a consistent and quality service that they can rely on.

Where you shop is your decision. It must be based on a combination of quality, cost and convenience. When you first take over it is easier to follow the previous owners' example until you have found your feet.

We continually discuss and monitor the purchases of provisions and we take into account the cost and quality. If we can find a product locally that is of the same or better quality we make a change. Even a 50p saving on an item you purchase every day represents a saving which could free up funds to spend on other areas.

Research

The tourist authority covering your location usually produces annual reports on the leisure activity and buying trends of tourists to your area. The reports will also include national and local occupancy levels. These can be a useful tool when preparing your initial business plan and when you are planning your marketing schedule.

It is not always obvious or easy to discover whether the advertising that you have paid for is actually making a difference. Some online services will provide you with feedback or give you the hit rate for your entry. They may also send you an e-mail each time there is a hit on your page.

One of the best indications is to ask your guests why they decided to make a booking with you and where they found out about you. If you ask every new enquiry this and do so consistently over a few weeks this will help you to build up a picture and decide on how to spend your budget in the future. It is important to continue with this and not to be put off when callers answer by saying they can't remember where they found out about you.

You should also monitor your competitors and look to see how the major hotels promote themselves. You will learn much from this.

Researching your local area will help you to plan ahead. If you are reliant on the holiday trade then researching the buying patterns of holidaymakers will help you to determine if more or less people are likely to take their holiday in your area, overseas or somewhere else in the UK. The weather is of course a major factor in this. If there has been an outbreak of a contagious disease that affects animals in rural areas, this may also play a part in the holidaymakers' decision. There might be areas of the country which become off limits for long periods.

A visitors' book at reception will give your guests the opportunity to give feedback and if they choose to they can do so anonymously. You might also consider asking your guests if there is anything they feel you could do to make their stay more comfortable. We do this with our regular customers when we are trying to decide if we should install a new service in each room.

Some hotel sites advertising accommodation include an option for guests to make comments about their stay at a hotel online. These can only be found by checking the internet on a regular basis.

Security

In a small hotel security is relatively straightforward to address. If you live on the premises you will be aware of which guests are in residence and where they are at any given time.

If a person walks into your hotel unchallenged and then stands at reception for any length of time waiting to be greeted and you do not respond you risk losing their business. If they are untrustworthy you risk much more.

We have heard from guests of instances when they have been left waiting at reception in a hotel for 15 minutes or longer. They have attempted to call the owner to no avail and decided to leave. It is doubtful that they will ever return.

If you are on-site most of the time you must be available to your guests. If you have to go out for any reason your guests and any visitors must have a method to contact you by. Leaving the hotel unattended when you are open for business is a risk.

We have a CCTV system monitoring our reception, bar area and car park. We are about to have a camera installed to cover the external view of the hotel including the front door. The system is discreet and most of our guests do not notice they are being watched. If you already have or decide to install CCTV externally you must consult with your local police force on the legality of the position of any camera.

There are many suppliers in the CCTV industry and few in our experience have managed to come up with a cost-effective solution for small businesses. If you plan to upgrade your existing system or to install a new one you must shop around.

We have met with companies who wanted to install cameras in every common area on the ground floor of the hotel. The cost proved to be well beyond our reach. With a small family-run hotel attracting regular customers it is not necessary to have cameras everywhere. You must consider the needs of your guests – they will not wish to be watched all of the time even if the technology is discreet.

Fire safety is a major concern. You must assess the risk of fire in your hotel as a matter of routine. Common sense is a good guide to fire safety and now that smoking has been made illegal the risk is reduced. You must make your staff aware of your policy on fire safety and it is advisable to brief any new guests staying for the first time to familiarise themselves with the building and the escape routes. You should also remind them that smoking is now outlawed.

You must re-visit your fire safety policy on a regular basis and ensure that you keep up to date with any regulations. This is easy enough to do and most fire authorities will advise you and have data available online.

In the case of an emergency you must follow your publicised drill and this must be practised at least once a year. We have a fire drill twice a year and brief our staff frequently. We test each fire alarm point once a month by rotation.

Smoking

From 1 July 2007 it became against the law to smoke in virtually any enclosed public place and in the workplace. This includes hotels. It is possible to designate one guest bedroom as a 'smoking' room. However, if you decide to do this you must, by law, ensure that any door opening from that room into a public space must close automatically to stop smoke polluting any area used by other guests or your workforce. If you have to install the appropriate mechanism this may well involve considerable expense.

With a small hotel, designating one bedroom for smokers will greatly reduce your turnover. Very few people ask for a smoking room – in fact in the first six months following the introduction of the new law, we have not had a single enquiry for this type of room.

Smoke alarms in each room are not usually sensitive to smoke from cigarettes. Guests who decide to smoke in their bedroom will pollute the atmosphere not just in the room but also in the immediate area outside of their room. Since the start of the new legislation it has become much easier to distinguish whether a guest is a smoker from the smell of their clothing.

Occasionally a guest that smokes will do so in their room. Some even tamper with the smoke alarm. We do not provide shower caps in our bathrooms as guests have been known to use these as a cover for the alarm. Others will unscrew the alarm. Your alarm system should alert you to this. Emptying waste paper bins every day will also signal if a guest has been smoking.

Staff

If you employ people to work for you, you must manage them fairly and with respect. It can be expensive and is time-consuming to look for a new employee. It takes time to get to know someone and to train him or her to work to your preferred standard. You will not have time to be continually training and advertising. You must do everything you can to make your place of work enjoyable for your staff. Investment in terms of time and effort in doing so will pay dividends.

If your staff are unhappy this will at some point become apparent to your guests. If they enjoy their work and look forward to coming in each day this will also be evident to anyone staying in or visiting your hotel. A happy workforce that stays with you for a long period will also work harder and be loyal and reliable.

We involve our staff in any decisions we have to make and when appropriate we ask them for their input. We encourage them to report any problems to us. They are aware of our attitude towards customer service and our expectations of them in this respect. Communicating with your workforce at all times will ensure that your hotel runs smoothly.

Suppliers

It will become obvious to you very quickly if one of your key suppliers is unreliable. You should not work with companies that let you down or that overcharge you. As soon as you become aware of a problem you must make it clear to the supplier that you are not happy with their service and the reason for this. You must be fair to them and give them the opportunity to address the problem and put things right.

If this does happen it is prudent to investigate alternative suppliers while you wait to see if your existing one improves to a satisfactory level. If they do not you will have another company waiting to step in and as a result you will enjoy an uninterrupted service.

There are plenty of companies that supply hotels and you will have a wide choice to select from, although changing a supplier remains a risk. Continually comparing different options allows you to make a decision quickly and without too much upheaval. It may also save you money.

Utilities

Paying your bills for rates, water, lighting and heating is unavoidable. They must be paid on time every month and normally by direct debit. You must factor this into your budget for each item. When you are in the process of buying your hotel you should ask the owner to furnish you with the relevant financial information pertaining to the cost of utilities supplied to the premises.

The tariff for rates and water are set each year. If you are taking over at the beginning of the year you must also find out by how much these will increase.

Gas and electricity suppliers will ask you to agree to a contract over a one- or two-year period. It is possible to shop around and there are commercial suppliers for these services who may be more cost-effective.

We pay for all of our utilities by monthly direct debit. When we receive an invoice we always check that we have not been over- or undercharged. We receive a visit every month by a meter reader but we still check the bill to ensure that the reading has been applied. If the bill is estimated we read the meter ourselves and call this in to the supplier and ask them to recalculate.

The utility bill each month is one of the major cost centres for a small hotel. Paying the correct amount each month will keep you up to date and will avoid the shock of receiving a huge bill out of the blue. You must remember to account for the fact that the cost will increase greatly over the winter months.

VAT

HM Customs and Excise offer numerous options to business customers and will explain these to you in detail. You must decide which of the options will suit your business the best. If you are registering for the first time your accountant may also be able to advise you on this.

You must account for VAT and pay this on time each time it is due. You must keep records of your accounts and a copy of any VAT return that you make.

We use the flat rate scheme. This saves us time and money. We simply pay a percentage of revenue rather than account for revenue and expenditure.

Your environment

The location of your hotel is vital. Finding out all about the local area surrounding your hotel is an important factor in your overall success. This is far reaching. It will allow you to assist your guests as they try to find their way around and become accustomed to the locality. It will help you discover the facilities available to guests and to yourselves. It will help you get to know other local businesses and your neighbours.

This not only allows you to give advice to guests on where to eat, which pubs to visit, where the best shops can be found, which tourist attractions are nearby, the nearest train or bus station or which taxi service to use, it also helps you to build local relationships.

When we first arrived at our new hotel we didn't know anybody in the area other than the outgoing owners. A year on we know hundreds of local people. This has helped us to settle into our new environment but has also attracted trade to the hotel. The first task I undertook on our arrival was to visit every shop, pub, restaurant and hotel in our street and introduce myself. Before we arrived we studied the local area and visited the hotel and town on eight occasions. This helped us to get a feel for the place. We checked out local amenities, visited schools, took lunch in a café, held a meeting with our building society in the pub

233

over the road from the hotel, studied local maps, took a drive to other nearby towns and did our very best to understand the way of life in our prospective new community.

On a regular basis I visit all of the other local business owners just to say hello and to discuss local issues. This is an excellent way of finding out more about the town and gives me an insight into what is happening and what people think.

Our town and the local area feature many events throughout the year and discovering when these take place gives a strong indication of when we will be busy. It also helps us to decide if we should advertise or run our own function to complement the forthcoming event.

Your website

Keep the hotel website up to date and consider refreshing the content every three to six months. If you offer a special rate at any time include this on the home page where it will be clearly visible to all visitors.

Most people have access to the internet. A professionally designed website is essential. Potential guests will visit your site and make a decision on where to stay based upon what they find.

If you are launching a new website show the design to as many of your friends and family as possible. Ask them for constructive feedback. Put yourselves in the position of a potential customer and decide if you would book a room based on the content of the site.

The layout must be clear and include your contact information in a position where it is easy to find. Include details of the local area and the facilities available. Your website should bring your hotel alive. It is a live, always available advertisement and must make your hotel an appealing prospect.

Notes

1. Main expenditure items to be accounted for:

   - Expenditure (overheads)
   - Bank interest
   - Cleaning
   - Insurance and telephone
   - Lighting and heating
   - Membership fees and finance charges
   - Miscellaneous
   - Motor expenses
   - Postage, stationery and advertising
   - Professional fees and licences
   - Rates and water
   - Repairs and renewals
   - Salaries
   - Staff costs
   - Total expenditure

2. Our response to and confirmation of a booking:

Dear [ ]

Thank you for your booking for a standard/superior double/twin room for single occupancy for the [date]. The room is en suite and the tariff of £[ ] per night includes bed and breakfast [and VAT].

If for any reason you have to cancel your stay with us please give at least 24 hours' notice. If we are unable to re-let your room we reserve the right to levy a cancellation charge for any cancellation received within 24 hours of your stay.

Please note that our hotel is now completely non-smoking in accordance with the new legislation effective from 1 July 2007. This includes all areas of the hotel. (Our bedrooms have always been non-smoking.)

I have detailed directions to the hotel below.

Please let me know if you require any additional information and we look forward to welcoming you to [name of hotel].

Kind regards

Proprietor

Directions: [hotel address and direction from nearest major road].

Car parking is available for residents at the rear of the hotel.

Index

A

A to Z 211
accommodation, own – separate 4
accommodation, own – live-in 5
accounting 59, 91, 212
advertising 144

B

bank account, choosing 57
bank account, managing 172–5
banking 101, 142, 213–14
bookings 142, 171, 215–17
breakfast 185–91
bricks and mortar 11
business plan 38–50
buying and selling 50–7

C

cancellation policy 217
cash flow 112
challenges 110
Chancel Repair 94
cheques 100
city centre location 9
cleaning 191
competition 15–16
complaints 218
countryside location 10
customer service 156–65

D

daily schedule 185

debit/credit card payments 99–100
diary of a hotelier 184–201
doubts 110

E

E-Mail 145, 167
emergencies 107–8
Estate Agent's fees 53
evening receptionist 200
events 219–21
experience, new tricks 109

F

facilities 170
finance options 35–8
financing 6, 33–5
fire safety 137
fixtures and fittings 53
food safety 138

G

goodwill 88
guests 22–5, 222
guests, questions 151–3

H

hotel grounds 129
hotel management 97–8, 147, 150–1, 180–2
housekeeping 221

I

insurance 54–6, 96, 223

invoices 101

L
laundry 122–4
licences 19, 96
local services, Fire Brigade 136
local services, the Police 135
location 4–6, 30–2, 97, 233

M
maintenance 12, 223
making a purchase, the final visit 73–81
making a purchase, your first visit 60–71
making an offer 82–96
making an offer, a reality check 83–6
making the move 103–6
managing communications 166
marketing 72–3, 102, 224
mortgage arrangement fees 53

O
occupancy 70–1
our story 202–10
overdraft 58
overseas location 10, 11

P
personal welfare 103, 176–9
practical advice 225
previous experience 2, 22
problem solving 23
professional fees and licences 226
provisions 227

Q
qualifications 16–18, 27

R
Radon Gas 94–5
registration forms 134
research 15, 227–8

routine 114
routine, afternoon 198–200
routine, daily 108
routine, morning 193–8

S
sales calls 153–6, 222
seaside location 8–9
security 229
selling the hotel, reasons for 90–1
selling your home 14
smoking laws 164, 230
solicitors' fees 52
staff 21, 132, 147, 231
staff, cleaning 149
staff, employing 72, 114
staff, getting along with 140
staff, kitchen 117
staff, leaving and new 118
staff, overseas 148
staff, paying 141–2
staff, problems 79–80
staff, reception 117
staff, teenage 119
staff, valuing 119
staff, wages 93
staff, waiting 149
staffing levels 115–16
Stamp Duty 52
stock taking 141
strengths and weaknesses 29
sundry costs 56
suppliers 103, 121–30
suppliers, deliveries 125–6
survey 11, 12
SWOT analysis 47–9

T
taking a break 111, 133, 177
technology 169
telephone 166–8, 213

U

unexpected, dealing with 113, 182–3
utilities 96, 232

V

valuation fees 52
VAT 101, 176, 233
viewings 7

W

way of life 28
website 102, 134, 143, 234
wholesalers 127
window cleaner 129

Y

your first few days as a hotelier 139
your first few days, planning 131–9
your first month 57
your own boss 20–1